JOURNEY IN WONDER

Slices of Abundant Life

WAYNE GRAHAM

DayStar BOOKS

Published by DayStar Books Ltd
PO Box 65275, Mairangi Bay, Auckland 0754

ISBN: 978-1-99-115391-3 (Softcover)
ISBN: 978-1-99-115393-7 (eBook)

All Scripture quotations, unless otherwise indicated, are from the New International Version of the Bible. Scripture quotations marked TPT are from The Passion Translation.

Sketches and Icons: Geneva Nevell

Print production by Outline Print Consultancy, New Zealand
eBook production by Castle Publishing Services, New Zealand

Contents

Foreword

BORN AGAIN

WONDER

Foreword

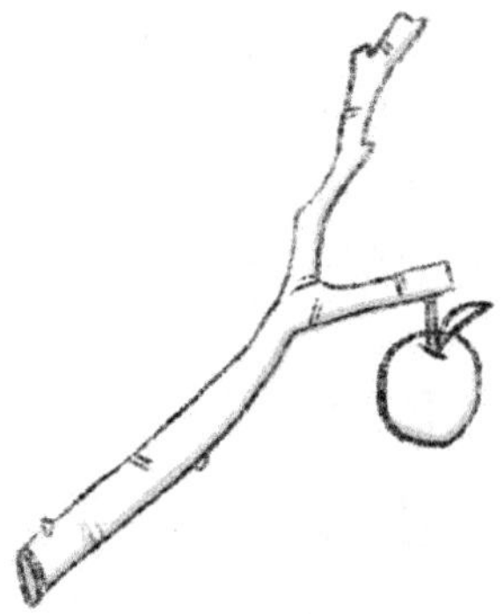

As I approached my mid-forties, having gone through a divorce and the loss of a very close friend through cancer, I started questioning the value of life.

The joy of having a high salary, with its accompanying perks of a company car, corporate box and business lunches, had begun to wane.

When I realised that I would be able to retire comfortably in ten years' time I asked myself, "For what purpose?" It seemed totally unfulfilling to be retiring to live a happy life just for me.

One of my assistant accountants went to church and I asked her if there was an *Alpha* course coming up. I had seen billboards around town. None were on the horizon but her church set up a course called *Journeys*, which showcased Christians living in faith.

On the second week of *Journeys* I watched a video about the miracle healing of a young, promising violin player. Her fingers had been crushed in a car door and she had been told by her doctor that she would never be able to play the violin again. A Catholic priest prayed for her injured hand and the video showed her healed and playing the violin again.

I found this video testimony particularly challenging. That night I cried out to God, asking that if he was real could he take away a painful verruca that had been on my right heel for three months.

The next morning I went to work and arrived home that evening to get ready to go for a bike ride. I had stopped running and taken up biking because of my painful heel. As I took my socks off to change into my biking gear I looked at my foot and noticed that the verruca was no longer there. It had completely disappeared, as well as the pain.

Was this from God or a coincidence? If it was from God I had to make a decision to give my life to him. I decided then and there to give myself one hundred per cent to God, which I've never regretted.

A whole new world opened up for me. Since becoming a Christian I have met so many beautiful, sacrificial people and travelled on mission trips to Asia, Africa, America and the Middle East, witnessing many miracle healings and the power of God.

This book tells of my journey in wonder with God and I hope the following stories will bring you encouragement, joy and hope.

Wayne Graham
February, 2022

BORN AGAIN

Doing what you do well builds a well.

1

A Tree Planted By The Water

I love to go for long walks up steep hills and through the bush. One of my favourite places for walking in Wellington, New Zealand, is Wilton Bush. It's sheltered from the wind and there are many tracks you can take, both long and short.

Depending upon the weather, I choose which way to walk – along streams, up steep steps, on shingled low gradient paths or through the mud. It is a beautiful place to listen to the birds and talk with God. I often use this time to write songs, free from the noisy clutter of the world.

On one particular track, halfway up a hill near a stream, is a tree that is extremely old. It stands tall, strong and proud behind a wooden sign that reads: Rimu - 800 years old.

I have pondered how this tree came to have such a long life. How many birds have sung in its branches and how many seedlings have sprung from it?

I can only assume that it found itself in an ideal position for growth, sheltered from the wind, blessed with good water, sun, and rooted in rich soil.

A tree grows by absorbing the nutrients from the soil. In the same way, a person is blessed by yielding to God and being careful about his/her surroundings, as described in Psalm 1.

Blessed is the one
who does not walk in step with the wicked
or stand in the way that sinners take
or sit in the company of mockers,

but whose delight is in the law of the Lord,
and who meditates on his law, day and night.
That person is like a tree planted by streams of water,
which yields its fruit in season
and whose leaf does not wither—
whatever they do prospers.

We are taught that spending time with God, reading and meditating on the Scriptures, and praying is important for a godly life. So is surrounding ourselves with godly friends and mentors and having a good church home group.

We are not called to live isolated from the world, but need to live *in* the world. Mixing with non-believers and having a kingdom influence in the market place is important.

Let me give some practical examples of what living in the world can look like from a Christian perspective.

Socialising with workmates

When I became a Christian I had to make a decision about whether I would still socialise with my workmates.
During the rugby season we would head down to the pub on a Friday night and watch the Super 12 games over a good number of beers. I made the decision that it was important for me to keep socialising with my colleagues, but in a slightly more refined manner.

Instead of drinking eight to ten beers every Friday night I limited myself to two beers. This became rather obvious to my workmates as it was traditional to buy each other a round, and there was some peer pressure to consume the beers quickly.

During the course of the night one of my colleagues questioned me on why I was only buying beers for them and not for myself.

I explained, "Since I have become a Christian I feel this sense of peace and contentment I didn't have before. I am worried that if I have more than two beers I will lose it."

This explanation was accepted and it was never a problem again.

Drawing a circle around what makes you content

Before I became a Christian I was caught up in the material ways of the world, always looking to find a better house, a trendier car or stereo system, or an overseas trip. The more money I had the more I wanted to spend.

After I became a Christian I found more joy in giving than accumulating and realised that everything I owned belonged to God.

I sense a peace and contentment I didn't have before.

I discovered that when I gave to others God blessed me in unexpected ways. This was not my motive for doing it, but by to others my life became more rewarding.

In Proverbs 11:25 we read: *A generous person will prosper; whoever refreshes others will be refreshed.*

One thing I find helpful is to draw a circle around what makes me feel content.

For example:

- » What is your ideal house?
- » What is your ideal car?
- » How much money do you need to live on?
- » What gives you joy that does not cost money?

By drawing a circle around what makes you content as your salary grows, your lifestyle expectations won't, and you might find you have more money to give to others.

Free from burdens

I believe that a key to an abundant life is holding no grudges and being able to forgive people.

Many times in my life I have experienced hurt and disappointment. When I became a Christian I realised I could free myself from such things by passing them over to God.

He knows what I am going through. He knows the truth behind everything that has happened. By passing them on and forgiving those who caused the hurts I am able to free myself and move on, always trusting that God will bring all things to light in time.

Cast your cares on the Lord and he will sustain you; he will never let the righteous be shaken (Psalm 55:22).

Furthermore, as Christians we have an even higher calling. As well as forgiving people we are called to bless them. This can be a very difficult thing to do and is often the opposite of how we feel.

One of the greatest examples of blessing those who have hurt us is in the parable of the lost son (Luke 15:11-32).

A loving father's youngest son demands his inheritance early and the father grants his request. His son sets off for a distant country, squanders the money in wild living and, in desperation, returns to his father, destitute.

The father, instead of being angry with his son, welcomes him back with open arms, and blesses him with his best robe and a fattened calf.

The father was joyful that his son, who had been lost, was now found.

A tree of contentment

I imagine the 800-year-old tree lies there content, familiar and happy with its surroundings, drawing nutrients from the soil, free from bitter roots that stifle life.

This is how I want to live – a life full of thankfulness and contentment, as Paul describes in Philippians 4:12: *I know what it is to be in need, and I know what it is to have plenty. I have learned the secret of being content in any and every situation, whether well fed or hungry, whether living in plenty or in want.*

2

The Quest For Perfection

My father was bald. So was my grandfather on my mother's side. I wonder if my new grandsons will inherit this trait.

When I was in the fifth form (Year 11) our science teacher told us that if your father was bald, and your grandfather on your mother's side was bald, there was a hundred per cent chance you would also become bald.

Science had struck a cruel blow.

I first noticed this in my late twenties. When I showered and washed my hair there would be a pile of black hair at the bottom of the shower cubicle.

In my mid-thirties I started trying to comb it over. I could hide my receding hairline by spreading my hair from the left side of my head up and over my bald spot.

This worked well when I was inside, but was highly ineffective in Wellington, the windy city where I lived.

The reckoning

One day I noticed a middle-aged man with the ultimate comb-over.

He had a part in his hair that started from beneath his ear lobe and spread out to a greasy matted pile of hair over the top of his head. It looked ridiculous.

I asked myself if this was how I wanted to look in the future. It didn't take me long to say no.

Then I made the decision. I had my first number two haircut and felt an exhilarating freedom. I no longer had to hide the real me, and felt more comfortable in my own skin.

I could walk confidently, whether I was inside or outside, in total freedom, without the worries of the comb-over.

Becoming a believer

When I became a Christian I had another epiphany.

I began to understand that God really loved me for who I was as his child. I didn't have to compare myself to anyone else.
I could see him looking down on the world, watching all these tiny black, grey, brown and blonde specks. He looked down on me and saw a tiny, shiny bald speck.

I was special.

I was unique, baldness and all.

I praise you because I am fearfully and wonderfully made;
Your works are wonderful I know that full well.
My frame was not hidden from you when I was made in the secret place.
When I was woven together in the depths of the earth
(Psalm 139:14-15).

Each one should test his own actions. Then he can take pride in himself, without comparing himself to somebody else (Galatians 6:45).

It breaks my heart when I witness teenagers feeling inadequate about their appearance, because they dwell on minor body imperfections. Some young women see their only hope in plastic surgery, on a quest for never-ending cosmetic perfection. They think their worldly success is determined by how they look rather than who they are.

Very few people seem to measure success by the strength of one's character and tenderness of heart.

The perfect example

I have come to realise that the quest for perfection shouldn't be measured in worldly ways, but in being more like Jesus.

The more time we spend with him the more we will become like him.

The better we get to know him the better we will reflect him.

I've met some people who reflect this inner beauty. They are mature Christians who would be the first to admit they have not lived a perfect life but, over many decades, they have been moulded and refined by God to become more like Jesus.

They radiate warmth, call a spade a spade, have a good sense of humour and you always feel safe and validated around them. When you spend time with them you feel stimulated spiritually.

Becoming more like Jesus doesn't have to be a performance exercise based on how many minutes or hours are spent alone with him. It can start with this simple prayer at the beginning of each day: "Lord help me to spend this day loving you and carrying out your will."

Every good and perfect gift is from above, coming down from the Father of heavenly lights, who does not change like shifting shadows (James 1:17).

3

The Power Of Your Story

I had many friends who were non-believers.

Many of them found it hard to fathom that I had found God. Some assumed I needed a crutch and that was my reason for finding the church. Others felt that I would soon get over it and return to my normal life.

In my favour I had a powerful personal testimony about the miracle healing of my foot. However, I still felt I needed to justify my faith to my non-Christian friends.

To prove I was not foolish I embarked on a mission to study creation and evolution and find some good scientific answers to any questions my non-Christian friends would pose about God.

I discovered some startling facts and new scientific terms, such as 'irreversible complexity'. This describes creatures that defy evolution. In other words, creatures created so complex from day one that they could not have evolved.

For example, a dolphin finds its food through a sophisticated sonar radar system. If the dolphin's sonar radar system had not fully functioned from day one it would have starved.

Once I understood more about creation and evolution from a God perspective I became comfortable that creation, evolution and science were quite compatible with the existence of a one-creator God.

And God said, "Let the water teem with living creatures, and let birds fly above the earth across the vault of the sky." So God created the great creatures of the sea and every living thing with which the water teems and that moves about in it, according to their kinds, and every winged bird according to its kind. And God saw that it was good (Genesis 1:20-21)..

This knowledge gave me good answers to any of my friends' challenging questions. I could prove to them that I was not deluded.

Ironically, once I had all this validation available the need for it faded away.

I realised it was my personal testimony that carried the greatest weight. No one could discredit my personal testimony. It was my truth.

Sharing my testimony

Recently, I caught up with an old friend with whom I had lost touch. We hadn't seen each other for twenty years.

Twenty years is a long time and it was wonderful to share together what had happened over the years. I told him that I had become a Christian.

He was not fazed by this and shared he had a faith too. He believed not just in one God but in many Gods. Living a good life was important to him.

Lately, however, his life has gone downhill, following a relationship break-up. He is now reaching out to old friends, reconnecting with me through the internet.

As I listened to him sharing his story and his pain I thought about how much he needed Jesus. He asked me how I became a Christian.

I told him my personal testimony about searching for a purpose in life and how God had healed a painful verruca on my heel.

My friend, who up to that point had been very upset and angry with life, looked at me in astonishment, smiled, put his hand on my shoulder and responded, "Well, Wayne, that is your testimony? No one can take that away from you."

God, if you are real, remove this painful verruca.

After we parted later that night I prayed for him and cried out to God for him.

A few days later he phoned me. His circumstances had become even more desperate. After empathising with him I asked him if I could pray for him right then in the name of Jesus. He willingly accepted.

This brought me a great deal of pleasure and reminded me that our personal testimony is powerful. It opens doors, softens hearts and cannot be repudiated.

Another example happened a few years ago when I was due to go on an overseas mission trip to Turkey with a group from Hamilton.

I knew only one person making the trip, the leader. Because most of us were strangers we decided it would be a good idea for us to get to know each other before the trip. So I flew to Hamilton to meet them.

We spent the first two hours just sharing our testimonies about how we came to know the Lord. It was extraordinary how sharing our testimonies brought us together and bonded us. We left the room no longer strangers, but brothers and sisters.

With great power the apostles continued to testify to the resurrection of the Lord Jesus. And God's grace was so powerfully at work in them all (Acts 4:33).

4

Playing With Soft Hands

The founder of the Vineyard Church movement, John Wimber, wrote a book called Everyone Gets to Play. John believed that the miracles Jesus performed in the Bible could still be performed by us today.

He also believed that following Jesus was not a spectator sport. He was more interested in his relationship with Jesus than in religion, and how it impacted on his life and others.

I, too, have discovered that playing in the kingdom of God is different from the ways of the world. It's a bit like a game of golf, which is different from other ball sports I have played.

I am reasonable at most ball sports. I have a gold medal for table tennis from the Olympics at Club Med in Tahiti.

Yes, this was just a social tournament, but I still had to beat a number of other entrants to make the final, where I met a young American man and beat him. He wasn't happy to be defeated by an older Kiwi.

God has given me good hand-eye coordination. If you hit a ball to me I am pretty good at hitting it straight back, but when it comes to golf I am absolutely hopeless.

Golf is different – the ball is not coming at you.

The little ball is sitting there waiting to be hit. It's just me and that little ball, and too much time to think about hitting it.

A game of opposites

Golf is a game of opposites. The softer you try and hit the ball the further it goes. It is all about timing and it's not about your own strength.

The last game of golf I played was with my late uncle. He had been playing every week and was getting coaching lessons. I hadn't played golf for about a year. I went first, on the first tee.

Because I had such low expectations about how far I could hit the ball and in which direction, I just swung through softly. By total fluke the ball travelled 200 metres perfectly straight down the middle of the fairway.

My uncle badly sliced his first shot and ended up 150 metres in the rough. His second shot was fairly ordinary, landing a decent distance from the hole. My second shot was average, but on the edge of the green. My uncle's third shot was as good as my second shot and the ball positioned about 30 metres from the green.

I was on the green in two shots with a chance for a birdie, while my uncle had already played his three shots and was heading for a bogey five. I stood on the green behind the flag in pride as my uncle played his fourth shot from 30 metres away.

What happened next was amazing. He played his fourth shot using a wedge. Now, I don't know if you know much about a wedge, but the aim is to lift the ball off the ground and let it fall gently onto the green with a bit of back spin.

Unfortunately, instead of getting underneath the ball my uncle topped it, hitting it with the wrong part of the club. Instead of the ball sailing up into the air and landing gently on the green it took off and came at me real fast. I had little time to get out of the way. It was flying at me, aiming to hit and hurt me, but just as I was bracing myself for the pain a miracle happened.

The ball hit nearly three-quarters of the way up the flagpole, rolling down the pole into the hole.

My uncle yelled out, "Par." I looked at him in total bewilderment and proceeded to three-putt.

Amazingly, he won the hole through a miracle of grace.

And I believe so it is with Christ.

A kingdom of opposites

The Bible says, *The last will be first and the first will be last* (Matthew 20:16).

We need to lose our life to save it. It's not about success and recognition. It's about humbling ourselves in service.

It's not about accumulating possessions. It's about sharing and community.

It's not what you have and what you wear on the outside. It's what you have on the inside that counts.

For we need not strive in our own strength. We can rely on God to guide us and give us strength.

It's easy to react to the world coming at you – the deadlines, the text messages, the problems. It's harder to concentrate on the one thing that matters, the most important thing.

It's not about possessions. It's about sharing and community.

It does not matter how good our first shot is. It is still easy to fall by the wayside and three-putt.

It's easy to muck up when you try and do things in your own strength, with hard hands rather than soft hands.

And it doesn't matter how many bad shots you've made in the past. It doesn't matter how far you're off the fairway. It doesn't matter how deep you are in the rough, or how difficult the bunker shot is.

God can work a miracle. He can find the hole through a miracle of grace, because he planned for us to succeed.

For I know the plans I have for you, declares the Lord, plans to prosper you and not to harm you, plans to give you hope and a future (Jeremiah 29:11).

We just lean on him and trust in him.

Trust in the Lord with all your heart and lean not on your own understanding (Proverbs 3:5)

5

Always There

A friend phoned me the other day.

As I was talking to her she asked me if I had seen the email she'd sent me. I told her I hadn't but would have a quick look.

I went searching around the house for my iPhone to bring up the email. I couldn't remember where I'd left it – not on the kitchen bench, the most obvious place.

I couldn't find it in the dining room, or my bedroom, or in the lounge. I looked in my bag and it wasn't there either. I was getting increasingly frustrated and annoyed.

Then I realised that I was talking to her on my iPhone! It had always been there, in my hand.

My children and family

When you have children, they are always there.

My eldest daughter lives in Australia and my son lives in Wellington. Despite the fact that I am now living in Christchurch the distance doesn't divide us.

They are always in the back of my mind, and we can get easily get in touch with each other through the marvels of technology.

They will always be there for me and I will always be there for them.

My youngest daughter, son-in-law and grandsons live close by. Being there for each other is only a five-minute drive away.

My parents have both passed away. Their legacy, however, lives on. I am constantly reminded of the values they passed on, almost as if their spirit lives within me.

My parents were always there for me and I plan to pass that legacy on to my children and grandchildren.

God

The experience and reflection above has helped me realise that God is always there. No matter what you are going through in life God is ever present.

He is in your joy and in your sorrow. He is in your completeness and in your brokenness.

There is nothing that I have been through that God, in the person of Jesus, has not experienced.

So often I have been guilty of going to God only in my sorrows and brokenness, turning to him only when I needed something or thought I needed something.

He is in your joy and sorrow, in your completeness and brokenness.

When life is good it has been easy for me to lose focus and let pride and fleshly desire take control. This has meant that I forget to praise him when things are going well, and don't recognise him in my accomplishments.

Also, there have been times when I am rushed by the busyness of life and fail to take the time to slow down and appreciate a special moment, or the Creator's beauty around me.

David thought about this too and cried out:

Where can I go from your Spirit?
Where can I flee from your presence?
If I go up to the heavens, you are there;
If I make my bed in the depths, you are there.
If I rise on the wings of the dawn,
If I settle on the far side of the sea,
even there your hand will guide me,
your right hand will hold me fast.
(Psalm 139: verses 7-10)

As I meditate on these verses I am astounded by the width and depth of the promises.

God is in our heavenly encounters, in our joyous moments, and he will cradle us in our lows.

No matter how far we journey he is there to guide us, hold us and appreciate us.

I want to live a life where God is at the forefront of everything I do, a life where he is ever-present in my thoughts and my decision-making, where I appreciate what I am holding within me and what has been placed around me.

The experience with my 'lost' iPhone has taught me a valuable lesson. It has reminded me of my relationship with God, that I cannot do anything worthwhile without him.

He is always there for me.

6

The Journey From Hell

Another occasion, when I was reminded that God is always there, was on an overseas trip with my youngest daughter a few years ago.

We found ourselves in a tricky situation and had to make a dicey decision. Was it going to be worth the risk?

We were stranded in Spain, both so sleep-deprived and exhausted that the only hope we had was in giving an affirmative answer.

It all began the night before on the Moroccan overnight train from Marrakesh to Tangiers. The first-class cabin I had booked was much less than expected. It contained no bunks, just bench seats. As the carriage filled up there was no room to lie down and sleep.

Just before departure the speaker in the carriage roared to life and let out a high-pitched scream, warning us that the train was about to move.

If you wanted to design a speaker to be the most aggravating speaker possible this one would 'take the cake'. If you wanted to design a speaker for hell this one would fit the bill.

It turned out to be a night from hell, indeed.

As the train moved it was impossible to start falling asleep. Every time we were about to doze off the speaker would roar to life, telling us we were close to the next station. It made us jump.

This went on all night. Thirty minutes before we were due to arrive in Tangiers I realised we needed to find a way to get from the railway station to the port where we would catch a ferry to Spain.

In desperation I cried out, "Does anyone speak English?"

An American voice spoke up and offered to help us catch a taxi from the railway station to the port of Tangiers. A short time later we found ourselves safely on the road to the ferry terminal.

The crossing to Spain proved uneventful and we looked forward to arriving in the Costa Del Sol where, according to TripAdvisor, we could get a bus to our hotel.

However, we found ourselves stranded on a footpath outside

the ferry terminal with no sign of a bus anywhere. We discovered they weren't operating that day, and our hotel was 90 kilometres away.

We stood there in a state of bewilderment.

After a short time a stranger offered to take us there.

"How much?" I asked.

"Seventy Euros," he replied. This seemed a fair price. There was no other option.

We had to walk two kilometres through the back streets, dragging our suitcases behind us, to his beaten-up old Peugeot.

It didn't look very roadworthy, but we were so exhausted we just hopped in. I had a passing thought: *Are we about to be kidnapped?*

As it turned out, the driver was quite helpful and friendly, arriving safely at our hotel in good time. We crashed on to our beds.

Trust in God

Sometimes you can be so tired and weary you just have to let go and put your trust in God.

I look back on that journey and reflect.

God was with us when my daughter and I were on the train.

God was with us when the speaker in the train screamed.

God was with us when I asked for help on the train.

God was with us when we were stranded outside the ferry terminal in Spain.

The Lord Almighty is with us;
the God of Jacob is our fortress. (Psalm 46:11)

And God provided a complete stranger to drive us from the ferry terminal to our hotel, in quick time.

Or was it a stranger?

Perhaps it was an angel?

7

Do What You Do Well

One morning, while on a mission trip in India, I believed I heard a word from God.

Because the word was so perfectly formed and profound I presumed it was from the Lord. I couldn't have thought of this by myself: *"Doing what you do well builds a well."*

That evening I was ministering to some young Indian University students due to go to engineering school.

They were concerned about God's plan for their lives and whether they should do mechanical or electrical engineering.

I shared the word I received that morning and told them to do what was in front of them well and God would honour that.

Doing what you do well builds a well.

Doing whatever they chose well would give them favour and create a reservoir they could draw upon to sustain themselves in the future.

It wouldn't matter whether they chose electrical or mechanical engineering, God would bless what they did, if they did it well.

This word gave those students great comfort. A spirit of confusion was replaced with a spirit of excellence and a renewed sense of purpose.

An example from my life

I started my career as an accountant, which was not very exciting, but I tried to do it well. Because I did it well other doors opened for me.

Eventually, I was able to delegate all the boring accounting tasks and move into areas of business that were more interesting.

I loved formulating strategy and building business plans. I got involved in some large investment business cases, restructurings, mergers and acquisitions, and I loved it.

Those opportunities wouldn't have opened up if I hadn't done basic accounting well.

Each success had created a well, like a water well, that I could draw upon to help me overcome challenges in the future.

When you are struggling to know what God's purpose is for your life there can be a simple answer.

Just do what is in front of you well. This will open doors for you and create a reservoir for success.

God's purpose for your life

A few years ago God spoke to me powerfully about setting up a new media vehicle in New Zealand called the *Daily Encourager.*

I strongly believed this was God calling on my life, so I left my job a couple of years later to pursue this assignment.

However, being in God's purpose for your life doesn't make life any easier. He doesn't outline every step and timing like a well laid-out project plan. Nor does he provide all the resources you think you need according to your timetable.

His plans and thoughts are much deeper.

For my thoughts are not your thoughts, neither are your ways my ways," *declares the Lord* (Isaiah 55:8).

God is more interested in the development of your character than whether you have met your key milestones or achieved your key performance indicators.

Each step forward is balanced with faith and risk, alongside fully relying upon, and trusting in, the Lord.

I find each day is still a mystery. I have made mistakes along the way and learned from them. As we walk in faith the problems don't get any smaller or the challenges any easier.

But I know that God is the 'better than' God. He always has something better for you than your plans.

And I have learnt a secret. If you do what is in front of you to the best of your ability and commit what you are doing to the Lord, how can you go wrong?

> *Commit your way to the Lord;*
> *trust in him and he will do this:*
> *He will make your righteous reward shine like the dawn,*
> *your vindication like the noonday sun.*
> (Psalm 37:5-6)

8

A Knock At The Door

My late father told a story of an incident in Christchurch when he was a teenager. The story demonstrates a lack of obedience and humility.

In 1941, during World War II, there was fear of a Japanese invasion of New Zealand and a blackout was put in place in coastal areas.

Street lighting was turned down and the windows of most homes were covered with black curtains, paint or paper.

An Emergency Precautions Scheme (EPS) was set up, in which my father was involved. They were tasked to make sure the blackout was upheld because Japanese planes were flying overhead.

One night, when my father was out scouting the neighbourhood, the army sergeant accompanying him saw a light shining in a local Christchurch home. My fourteen-year-old father was asked to visit it.

My father knocked on the door using a knuckle duster. EPS kids used knuckledusters to ensure the knock was heard as some homes didn't have a doorbell.

A woman came to the door and Dad told her, "You've got a light shining. You have to get it out. Don't you know the Japanese are coming ashore?"

A voice from the back of the house yelled out, "Who's that?"

"Some snotty-nosed kid is telling us to put out our light for blackout drill," she replied.

The couple ended up being quite discourteous. My father returned to tell the sergeant about the 'snotty-nosed kid' comment and how the couple declined to turn their light off.

The army sergeant clicked into action and marched to the house with his loaded rifle. Standing outside the house he fired three shots through the window and extinguished the light.

The couple were furious they had to pay to fix the damage.

They were severely reprimanded by the sergeant who asked them if they were spies. He reminded them of the consequences of their actions.

Obedience and humility

The couple's actions, in not responding to the need to maintain the city in blackout, showed a lack of obedience and humility.

First, they did not obey a decree from the Government. Second, they refused to listen to a fourteen-year-old kid.

This story got me thinking about my walk with God and my own obedience and humility.

How much am I listening to God?

How hard does God have to knock to get my attention?

Do I respond to a quiet tap, or does God have to use a knuckle duster to get my attention?

Do I sometimes treat God like a snotty-nosed kid who is getting in my way?

Do I want to get to a stage where I find myself in a dark valley before I humble myself before him.

Even though I walk through the darkest valley, I will fear no evil, for you are with me; you rod and your staff comfort me (Psalm 23).

Learning from not listening

One of the hardest examples I have learned from not listening to God happened a few years ago, when I was in the lift with a work colleague.

It was early in the morning and there were only the two of us in the lift. The work colleague was perspiring and struggling with breathlessness; extremely overweight. I felt the Holy Spirit nudge me to speak to him, but I didn't know him very well. For some reason I lost the opportunity and remained silent.

How hard does God have to knock to get your attention?

Two days later I discovered that this work colleague had died from a heart attack.

 I was absolutely shocked and felt a huge sense of guilt that I hadn't responded to the Holy Spirit's prompting.

It taught me a huge lesson and has determined me to respond whenever I feel the nudge or hear that still small voice again.

Responding to the small voice

A few years ago I was in the United States at a Vineyard conference. We were asked to prophesy over someone nearby whom we didn't know.

Behind me was a young American woman in her late 20s. We agreed that we would prophesy over each other.

She gave me some great words of encouragement and, as she was talking, I saw a picture of her serving and drinking cups of tea with cakes.

This picture seemed ludicrous. She was a young American woman who would not be interested in tea parties. Also, Americans usually drank coffee not tea and not from teacups.

However, I felt the Holy Spirit nudge me to give her this picture.

After I told her, she informed me she and her husband had been praying about setting up afternoon teas in their neighbourhood for Muslim women.

The picture gave her great encouragement.

This was another reminder to trust God and not let physical circumstances undermine what is happening in the Spirit.

Humbling myself before God

To ensure I am walking with God I sometimes find the best thing to do is pray like this:

God, what are you up to today? What surprises do you have in store for me? Help me to do your will.

Perhaps, as we bow to God and give him each day, we can gravitate from the school of hard knocks to the school of blessings.

We come before the one who is gentle and humble in heart who lifts our burdens from us.

Come to me, all you who are weary and burdened, and I will give you rest. Take my yoke upon you and learn from me, for I am gentle and humble in heart, and you will find rest for your souls. For my yoke is easy and my burden is light (Matthew 11:28-30).

WONDER

Nothing is too small and nothing is too big for God

9

The Miracle Of The Lost Letter

There have been times in my life when I have had to question where I am with God. Am I still walking in his will for my life?

And there have been times when I have felt really disappointed about something that has occurred, when God has suddenly turned the situation around. This happened a few years ago. I was embarking on a new calling in my life, heading overseas on a four-week mission trip to China and India.

Before I left I felt I should visit some dear friends in Whanganui, to get their thoughts on my new calling – *Daily Encourager*.

When I arrived I found my friend Marian had been praying for this. She gave me many words of wisdom and encouragement.

It was going to be hard to remember everything she said so I asked her to email them to me. As she was in her mid-70s she preferred to send me a letter.

A week later, three days before I was due to fly to China and India, the letter arrived. It was beautifully hand written on parchment paper, full of wise counsel and encouragement. They were words I would want to re-read many times for they would guide and encourage me on my journey.

I was so excited that I phoned a mutual friend and shared the letter over dinner with her that night.

The following morning I went off to work. I had this vague recollection of putting the letter in my briefcase, but I searched in vain and couldn't find it.

When I got home that night I searched all around my house and still couldn't find it. Then I remembered I'd given it to my friend to read over dinner, so I phoned her to see if she had it. No luck.

I felt I should let Marian know how precious her letter was to me, so the next day I phoned her to thank her and confess I'd lost it.

I was hoping that Marian might be able to recreate the letter and send me another copy, but that didn't come up in our conversation. Disappointed, I felt that the enemy had snatched the letter from me.

All I could do was ask God for the letter to be found. As I flew out of the country that night I left the matter in his hands.

The trip to China and India was very rewarding. I had completely forgotten about the letter by the time I returned to Wellington four weeks later.

Awaiting me was the usual pile of mail and I noticed a letter from Marian. I thought she must have sent me another copy but when I opened the envelope I found her original letter with two notes.

The first one was from Marian and the second from Denise.

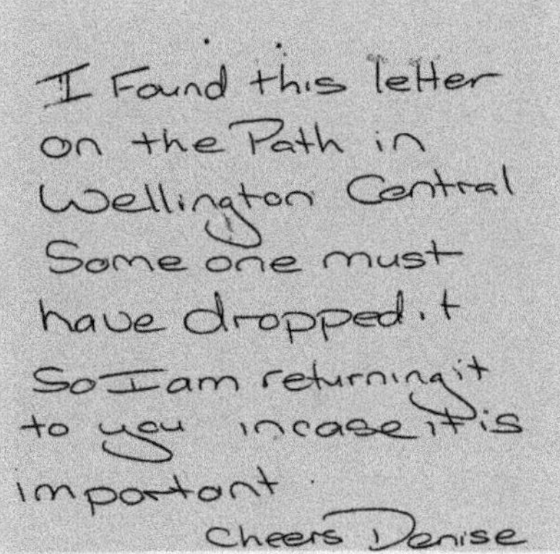

I found it amazing that the letter had been blowing around the streets of Wellington and someone was vigilant enough to pick it up and send it back to Marian.

She had received it more than two weeks after I'd lost it and friends have told me that it was raining in Wellington over that time. The fact that the letter arrived back in my hands in perfect condition was a miracle in itself.

Not wanting to push my luck I have carefully filed the letter away and scanned a copy to make sure it was preserved. I know that in the future I'll refer to it many times for encouragement.

This incident has taught me that God has his hand over every aspect of our lives. He protects both what is important to him and what is important to us.

Therefore, I tell you, do not worry about your life, what you will eat or drink; or about your body, what you will wear. Is not life more than food, and the body more than clothes? Look at the birds of the air; they do not sow or reap or store away in barns, and yet your heavenly Father feeds them. Are you not much more valuable than they? (Matthew 6:25-26)

10

Burning Burdens

The weight of responsibility of being a church home group leader was resting heavily on my shoulders.

I was six months into the role and the list of prayer requests was rapidly increasing. What started off as a list of three or four prayers had quickly turned into a list of over twenty. There were so many needs.

I had to pray for my children, who did not know Jesus, for members of my home group with health and job issues, other members of the church in need of prayer, and for our city.

As I worshipped at the back of the church one Sunday morning, my friend Dave, who is quite bold and discerning, approached me from behind. He exclaimed, "God says you have pebbles in your pockets and you need to get rid of them."

I turned and looked at him.

It didn't take me long to realise that the pebbles could be the prayer burdens I was carrying. So, in a prophetic act, I pulled my pocket linings out of my trousers and pretended to empty the pebbles onto the floor.

At the end of the service I still felt I needed some prayer so I approached the prayer team and told them my story.

A member of the team, Tim, felt God wanted me to list all my burdens on a piece of paper and have them burned. He offered to do that for me.

It seemed like a good idea, so I headed over to the church altar and proceeded to write out a list which I handed to Tim, folded over for confidentiality, and went home.

Later that afternoon Tim texted me that the list had been burned. I felt a sense of release, that a burden had been lifted as I left the prayers in God's hands.

I knew, however, my approach to prayer in the future would have to change.

Here and now

Today, my prayers are much less regimented, more spontaneous, intuitive and strategic.

I'm not good at writing and praying from a prayer list. I'm not good at remembering all prayer needs. Nor am I good at praying repetitive-type prayers. It's easy to get bored.

Now, when someone asks me for prayer, and this happens often, I tend to adopt a 'here and now' approach and be led by the Holy Spirit.

Often, I sense the need to pray for something during the day and sometimes during the night. When this happens I tend to stop what I am doing, focus, sense what God is saying and then pray. Once I have prayed I often feel a sense that something has moved in the Spirit.

And I no longer believe in long prayers. Before I pray I ask God what is on his heart and the prayer will be short, sharp and sweet.

Sometimes I have been astonished by the answers to prayers after what I thought were the weakest ones.

This happened once with my friend Carlie. She had been suffering for many years from a painful verruca on her foot. She had tried medical intervention, including incision, to try and get rid of it, yet nothing worked.

Even the weakest prayers are answered.

She knew that God had healed me of my verruca and asked me to pray for her.

That evening I prayed the most insipid of prayers. The next day Carlie told me she had been completely healed. The verruca has never returned over the fifteen years since.

Some people believe you have an anointing from God to heal

others when you have been healed yourself. What God has done before he will do again, to bless others.

I am a fellow servant with you and with your brothers and sisters who hold to the testimony of Jesus. Worship God! For it is the Spirit of prophecy who bears testimony to Jesus (Revelation 19:10).

Praying for mechanical items

Today, my prayers are not just limited to people. Sometimes I have prayed for broken mechanical items and seen them miraculously fixed.

This happened with my washing machine and my car, but one of the funnier moments was with a cheap toaster.

My friend John was staying with me for a couple of weeks while he was recovering from an operation. He was becoming increasingly annoyed with my toaster. It worked well with two slices of bread, but when we put in one slice of bread the toaster would eject the finished toast onto the floor.

I had tried to solve the problem, to no avail. I had lived with it by either intercepting the toast before it hit the floor or putting in two slices of bread instead.

This was not good enough for John. He said, "I think this toaster has a demon."

I responded, "I think you're right," and proceeded to pray over the toaster, commanding the demon to go in Jesus' name and for the toaster to work properly.

Nothing happened for a minute or so. Then I saw a picture of an arm inside the toaster. I felt God was telling me to have a look inside it, so I picked it up and turned it upside down.

I have the mechanical intuition of an accountant. It is highly unlikely that I can fix anything.

Led by the Spirit I found this arm inside the toaster and bent it. After that, the toaster worked well for another eighteen months before it finally gave up the ghost.

These days I never hesitate to pray for broken mechanical items. Sometimes prayer works, and sometimes wisdom prevails and I feel led to replace the item or have it fixed by an expert.

God seems personally interested in everything we do. He loves to be involved and help us make wise decisions.

Do not be anxious about anything, but in every situation, by prayer and petition, with thanksgiving, present your requests to God. And the peace of God, which transcends all understanding, will guard your hearts and your minds in Christ Jesus (Philippians 4:6-7)

'Do not be anxious about anything'. It doesn't say, 'Do not be anxious about most things'.

Nothing is too small and nothing is too big for God.

11

The Wonder Of The Flying Fish

A friend of mine once shared an amazing story about his father, and an enchanting fishing trip he went on in the early 1960s, while on a remote Pacific Island.

My friend's father was serving as a technical missionary in the New Hebrides (now Vanuatu) and had to install a pedal radio transmitter on an isolated island.

The British Government had installed pedal radio weather stations on two outer islands, Aniwa and Futuna, but those had failed.

The Government had retrieved and repaired them, but they needed someone to re-install them and ensure the systems were up and running. He had these skills.

However, the only access to the islands was by sea, and ships going to there were rare. He discovered that an Australian school teacher was going to the island of Futuna to examine the senior school children to assess them for college entry, so the government asked him if he would travel with her.

They arrived safely at Futuna and, after the teacher and he had finished their work, the village was elated. All their senior students passed and the weather station was operational again.

To celebrate, the village chief said they would have a feast on the beach for the evening meal but they would need to catch some fish first.

The teacher and technical missionary were asked if they would like to go on the fishing trip. They agreed, after taking a look at the canoe. It was a relatively large outrigger and obviously very seaworthy.

They sailed out nearly two miles offshore, at which time they came to a standstill in the pitch black.

One of the fishermen had a long pole on the end of which were tightly-bound 60-centimetre long pandanus leaves. He proceeded to light the top-most protruding leaves and held the glowing torch light high above him while standing.

The fishing crew heard movement in the waters around the canoe but didn't see anything. Then after a short time, flying fish leapt from the water. Some hit the canoe and dropped back into the water. Others flew over it. However, as more came to the light many fell into the canoe.

It wasn't long before the fisherman concluded there were enough fish to feed the village and the two guests.

Once ashore, the fish were processed and baked in a fire on the beach.

The locals had home-made bread and other cooked vegetables to add to the meal, which was washed down with a very pleasant green tea.

My friend's father and the school teacher experienced first-hand the warmth and friendliness of the village people, and a unique way of catching fish.

The wonder

There is much wonder in this story.

First, the wonder of miraculous provision. A fishing trip with no rods or bait – fish simply being attracted and caught by the light.

I have witnessed God's miraculous provision many times. This has ranged from small things like finding car carks and buying items that were heavily discounted, to bigger things like the multiplication of food, and money appearing in my bank account.

God can provide in unexpected ways and sometimes his timing seems last minute but I know that God is good and never late.

For my thoughts are not your thoughts, neither are your ways my ways,' declares the Lord (Isaiah 55:8).

Second, this story has parallels to our walk with Jesus.

If a small light on a boat is able to attract dozens of flying fish imagine how many people we can attract by bearing the light of Jesus. In a dark world do we truly appreciate how much we carry as his followers?

The light was much more effective in the darkness. If they had gone fishing during the day they would not have caught any fish after lighting the pole.

The light shines in the darkness, and the darkness has not overcome it (John 1:5).

I also found it fascinating that some fish landed back in the water and some scraped the side of the boat. Does this not parallel our own evangelism?

We can never expect a one hundred per cent success rate. On hearing the word of God some people will either walk away or only follow Jesus for a short time.

I also wonder what happened to the fish which didn't land in the boat? Did they end up swimming aimlessly in the ocean for the next few years?

And what happened to the fish that landed in the boat? Their great sacrifice brought much pleasure to the island people and their guests. Isn't this what fish were designed for?

In the same way, our lives are to be a sacrifice to God to bring him pleasure. Jesus set the prime example.

He is the atoning sacrifice for our sins, and not only for ours but also for the sins of the whole world (1 John 2:2).

12

Precise And Perfect Provision

God's provision can come in unexpected ways. I have been in situations where I have experienced God's favour and abundance, and I have been in situations where I have experienced the lack of them.

However, I've only been in one situation where God's provision was precise and perfect. This happened a few years ago when I was booked to go on a mission trip to Turkey with a group from the World Evangelism for Christ (WEC).

Many people in our tour group were students with limited funds, so we had to come up with a fundraising idea to raise enough money so everybody could travel. Despite selecting the cheapest travel routes we each had to find $3,000 to fund our three-week tour. This was a considerable amount of money for the fifteen students.

Fortunately, I was in full-time work and able to fund the cost of the trip myself. I was keen, however, to help as many of the others as possible.

To raise funds we designed a T-shirt and each one of us was expected to sell these through our networks, for $25 each. For three weeks I touted T-shirts at my local church and sold over twenty. With one week to go before the funding deadline I was a bit reluctant to get up in front of my church again. I thought people would be getting sick of me, but decided to give it one last push. To my surprise I managed to sell almost double what I had sold previously.

One person who had just become a Christian wanted a shirt but didn't have any cash on him, so he promised to drop a cheque around to my house that afternoon.

With some joy I reported the success to my friend Caleb in Hamilton who was organising the fundraising. He told me we were still $2,150 short of the overall fundraising target so, unfortunately, one student would miss out. I was disappointed but there was nothing else I could do.

An hour or so later the new Christian arrived with his cheque in a sealed envelope. I thanked him for his support and gave him his shirt.

After he had left I thought I'd better open the envelope and get the cheque ready for banking on Monday. I was stunned. Immediately, I phoned my friend in Hamilton.

"Hey, Caleb, guess what? Everybody will be able to go on the trip."

He was startled. "What do you mean?"

"Someone has just handed me a cheque of $2,150 for one T-shirt," I explained.

Caleb couldn't believe it either. He was over the moon with excitement and couldn't wait to tell the others.

Later that afternoon I phoned the new Christian. "Do you realise you have just given me a cheque of $2,150 for one T-shirt?"

"Yes," he replied, "That is what God told me to do."

"Well," I said, "it just so happens that this was the exact amount we needed to fund the trip for every student. Not a penny more or a penny less."

The new Christian was amazed. I thanked him once again for his gallant generosity and wished him all the best. I imagine as a new believer this was a big moment for him in his faith journey. He had clearly heard from God.

I still find it incredible today that God could orchestrate such a precise provision at the eleventh hour. But I guess he is a God in control, holding everything together in his hand.

He is before all things, and in him all things hold together (1 Colossians 1:17).

We had a wonderful time on our trip to Turkey and there was a plan and purpose for everyone.

God's perfect will prevailed.

13

The Hall Came Tumbling Down

Our old church hall had been standing for close to one hundred years. Once a place of honour, now it sat abandoned and dilapidated, a faded echo of its vibrant past. There were rumours that the only thing holding it together was the borer, holding hands.

Rusty sheets of roof iron and blistered weatherboards highlighted years of neglect, as the church pursued plans to knock it down and build a replacement.

For decades our Wellington-based church had a vision for a much bigger hall to meet our growing needs, to sit alongside the main church building. At every step, however, our efforts had been fraught by objections from neighbours about the size and design of the new hall and the effect it would have on surrounding properties.

It was now a health and safety risk and unhabitable. Time had run out. After countless years of faithful prayer, including all-night prayer sessions and the receiving of many encouraging prophetic words, there was still no green light.

To counter neighbourhood objections the church had invested considerable time and money on a new plan that was less intrusive on the neighbours, but the objections remained.

One night our home group focussed on the problem. As we prayed I was reminded of Joshua's strategy in conquering the city of Jericho. Feeling a nudge from God I suggested we immediately drive over to the old hall and march around it seven times.

Everybody was excited. This was going to be a home group with a difference.

Expectantly we hopped in our cars and made our way over, marching in an orderly fashion around the old hall. We laughed, danced, sang and praised the Lord as we lapped the hall. After the seventh lap we let out a huge shout to the Lord.

When the trumpets sounded, the army shouted, and at the sound of the trumpet, when the men gave a loud shout, the wall collapsed; so, everyone charged straight in, and they took the city (Joshua 6:20).

Anybody watching from the street would've thought we were completely mad but, as we finished our mission, we felt a sense of breakthrough. Something had moved in the Spirit.

A few weeks later the resource consent was finally granted and the neighbours' objections mitigated. Some sacred parts, including a stained-glass window, were carefully removed so they could be incorporated into the new building as a reminder of the past.

The construction of the new hall could begin. Did our marching around the hall and shout to the Lord make a difference? Was it the straw that broke the camel's back?

We laughed, danced, sang and praised the Lord.

I can never be sure, but I know that shortly after the new hall was completed there was a massive earthquake in Wellington.

The resulting destruction meant the main brick church, where services were held, could no longer be used. It was now a serious earthquake risk.

Today, the new hall is the place where the services are held and the brick church lies dormant, awaiting funds for earthquake strengthening.

God's timing was perfect.

This story is a reminder that when I am faced with an obstacle in my life, instead of continuing with the same old, same old, perhaps I need to turn to God for a new strategy.

If God could give Joshua a unique strategy to conquer Jericho he can give me a fresh strategy to knock down the walls in my life.

14

A New Hall Rises

The story behind the funding of the new hall displayed a remarkable move of God and significantly strengthened my faith.

Planning for the design of the new hall had taken many months and I had been asked to join the building committee at an early stage. This was the type of project I relished, having been involved in many building projects during my time as business manager at Fairfax. I loved being involved in building design.

At the first meeting of the building committee we already had 1.5 million dollars in the bank. This had accumulated from donations from faithful All Saints' parishioners over the decades.

We initially talked about limiting the building budget to this amount but 1.5 million dollars would only enable us to build a small barn-like structure that would hardly be inspirational to meet the growing needs of the church.

After some discussion we all agreed that we needed to have a much bolder vision, and come up with a design that met both the current and future needs of the church. This required faith that we could raise additional funds.

Working with the architects we ended up designing a beautiful new hall at an estimated cost of 2.3 million dollars. This meant we would need to find another eight hundred thousand dollars to enable the building project to proceed.

I felt convicted that I should make a good contribution towards this, given I had been instrumental in pushing for a bigger and more expensive hall. So, I thought I would give ten thousand dollars to the building project. Then I heard God say, "I don't want you to give ten thousand dollars. I want you to give one hundred thousand dollars."

With a little bit of nervousness I responded, "Okay God, but how do I find one hundred thousand dollars?"

Over the next day or so a plan came into my head.

First, there had been a recent change in the tax laws and the ability to claim a rebate on donations had been increased from a limit of two thousand dollars every year, to the total of your annual income.

This meant that I didn't have to find one hundred thousand dollars. I only needed to find sixty-seven thousand dollars as I could claim a 33% tax rebate on these donations.

Second, I realised I could find this money by reducing my mortgage payments over a period of time. By changing my mortgage to 'interest only' and reducing my mortgage payments by fifteen hundred dollars a month I would be able to find sixty-seven thousand dollars over four years.

One of the building committee members was a little taken aback when I shared that I would give one hundred thousand dollars for the new hall fund. He asked, "Wayne are you sure you can do this?"

Effectively, I was delaying my mortgage repayment by four years. I was quite comfortable with it, but what happened over the next few months was astonishing.

After saying yes to God I received news that I had won a ballot to purchase some shares at a good discount in an oil company in which I had already invested.

I was able to purchase an additional one hundred thousand shares in this company at ten cents each, whereas the market price was twelve cents. I could immediately sell these shares and make a profit of two thousand dollars, if I so wished.

I went ahead with the share purchase and watched as the share price grew. Within a few weeks the share price had risen from twelve cents to eighteen. Two months later the share price was 25 cents and climbing, on news that the company had discovered a new oil field off the coast of China.

Three months later the share price had risen to 45 cents, and I realised that if I sold my total holding in the company I would have made a profit of sixty-seven thousand dollars. I thought about it but felt uncomfortable.

It seemed too easy. There was no sacrifice. It was much better if there was some sacrifice in the funding of the hall, so I did not sell them at that time.

… and walk in the way of love, just as Christ loved us and gave himself up for us as a fragrant offering and sacrifice to God (Ephesians 5:2).

Over the next few months the share price did drop back a bit, and I did eventually sell some of the shares to fund other people's mission trips, but I never used the profit on them to fund the new hall. It was funded from the delaying of principal payments on my mortgage by four years.

> *It seemed too easy. There was no sacrifice.*

I sensed God was demonstrating, "This is what I can do when you give."

Within a few months we had garnered a significant number of pledges for the new hall and I know my one-hundred-thousand-dollar contribution helped a great deal. However, we were still two hundred thousand dollars short of our target of 2.3 million dollars and, with the architect's drawings completed, we had to make a decision on whether to go to tender.

In faith we did, and four companies responded. There was quite a bit of difference between the highest tender and the lowest tender. The higher tenders were in the 2.3 million range, but the lowest one was for 2.1 million dollars. This was exactly the amount we had saved.

There was a cry of joy. We had enough funding for the new hall. The foundations could be laid and the construction could begin.

With praise and thanksgiving, they sang to the Lord:

"He is good;
his love toward Israel endures forever."

And all the people gave a great shout of praise to the Lord, because the foundation of the house of the Lord was laid (Ezra 3:11).

15

New Day Dawning

It never occurred to me that God would use me to write songs. Nobody is less qualified. I struggle to play a musical instrument and at primary school I was asked to mime rather than sing, such is my musical ability.

My song writing journey began one Sunday morning at church. I was singing in my usual low, quiet monotone while everybody else was singing loudly and joyfully. How I wished I could sing well, but I was too embarrassed to sing in public.

The belief that I can't sing began many years ago at primary school when I volunteered to join the school choir. The choir master had said at assembly that anyone who joined the choir would be given free chocolate. Motivated purely by a love for chocolate I had put my hand up.

After a couple of weeks of rehearsals the choir master noticed that something did not sound quite right. So, she asked us to sing individually. When she heard me she said, "Wayne I will tell you what. You can stay in the choir and you will still get chocolate, but I just want you to mime from now on."

As a ten-year-old kid this didn't really bother me. I was still getting chocolate, but these words about my inability to sing stayed with me for the rest of my life.

Decades later, on that Sunday morning at church, I'd had enough. I said to the Lord, "Lord, I would love to be able to sing." I knew it was not a problem for him to be able to improve my singing voice. However, he answered the prayer in a totally unexpected way.

A few weeks later I was at a worship conference in Te Aroha, and the international artist, Jason Upton, was leading the worship. As we were worshipping, I heard these words.

You came into my life
Turned my world upside down
You came into the room
And took me by the hand
Help me Jesus to climb the mountains
Help me Jesus to dance in the valleys
Help me Jesus to see above the clouds
As you transform me
Into your likeness

I knew these were the words to a song, but I wasn't sure what to do with them as I don't play a musical instrument.

When I arrived back in Wellington I told Tim, a talented musician friend of mine, about this and he graciously offered to help. Next Sunday after church he sat down at the piano with me and helped me compose a melody. After about 30 minutes the song came together and it sounded really good.

A few days later as I was biking around the Miramar Peninsula another song came into my head.

This time it had both lyrics and a melody.

> *Sometimes I feel incapable*
> *Sometimes I see impossible*
> *Sometimes I look unworkable*
> *But I know it is not Your will*
> *Sometimes I get impatient*
> *Sometimes I seem self-centred*
> *Sometimes I fear honesty*
> *But I know this is not Your way*
> *For I know there is a place*
> *Where Your love flows*
> *I know there is a place*
> *Where Your strength grows*
> *There is a river*
> *There is a river of love*
> *Where Your spirit dwells*

This felt really weird. Over the one-hour bike ride I had the lyrics and melody to a whole new song.

I wondered what to do. Did this song come from me or did it come from the Lord? I decided that if it had come from God then I had to honour it. I didn't want to lose what I had been singing so I sang it into my iPhone.

After that, it was like a dam burst and a river of songs flowed. I was getting a new song every week and Tim and I started meeting regularly to work on them. As the number of new songs grew, it was becoming difficult to keep up. At one stage I had to tell the Lord to turn the tap off. We couldn't maintain it. After a few months of working on the songs Tim and I both became rather busy and the composing fell away.

The Lord brings a New Age musician

In the meantime an Anglican Minister, John Daysh, had asked me to help him set up new healing rooms at the Wellington Cathedral.

Shortly after opening them a man called Rob Whelan turned up at the Cathedral in need of prayer. He was a talented musician who followed New Age principles, but he had seen the sign outside on the footpath saying, 'Jesus heals'.

Rob had lost his voice, had a gig coming up and was desperate to be healed. We invited him in, told him that Jesus heals and prayed for his voice to be completely restored.

The next week he came back to the healing rooms with the news that his voice had been fine at the gig. He asked us to pray for his auntie in the UK who had some serious health problems. Because she was overseas we also prayed over a prayer cloth which Rob sent to her. His auntie's health improved dramatically overnight and after she received the prayer cloth a few days later she was healed.

Rob had witnessed the miracle healing ability of God and after a few months of many return visits he gave his life to the Lord.

As we got to know each other I mentioned to him that I had these songs the Lord had given me. Rob suggested we get together sometime to work on them.

Birth of an album

Nothing happened for a few months. Then one Sunday morning Rob turned up at my local church and told me the Lord had sent him and wanted us to collaborate on the songs. Rob invited me around to his flat at 7pm the next day to start work on them. I was excited about this prospect but over the next few hours started to get cold feet.

I thought this could be so embarrassing. Rob was a semi-professional musician with some international recognition. He might think these songs were really naff.

I prayed, "Lord if this is not from you, please let it fall to the ground. Please take it away. And if this is from you what song do I give Rob to start with?"

I heard the Lord say, "Give him *The Vine*."

The Vine was the third song I'd received. I had woken up at 5.30 am one morning and heard the opening words: *It took me a long time to find the vine where His presence flows into mine.*

When I arrived at Rob's flat the next night he asked, "What have you got?"

I gave him the lyrics to *The Vine*.

Rob looked at the words and told me that for two years he'd had this melody floating around in his head but was unable to write lyrics for it.

Give him the vine.

He started playing the melody and singing the words to *The Vine* and they just clicked into place. Within twenty minutes we had the song completely finished. It was amazing. Rob had never completed a song so quickly before.

Over the next few weeks I introduced Rob to more of my songs, and he started introducing them into his gigs at the pub. Sometimes he would change the word 'Jesus' to 'freedom'. People confessed to him they had been impacted by the words.

I started getting new songs. The tap was turned back on and the river was flowing again.

Often, I would get lyrics during the day as I was walking through the bush or up the many hills around Wellington. Rob would turn up the next day at Capital Vineyard, hungry for another song, and I would have a fresh one for him.

Sometimes he would turn up with a new melody and I would have new lyrics. They fitted like a glove. Sometimes I would have the words and a melody and sing it to Rob. It astonished me that Rob could pick up on the melody from my singing and work out the chords.

As the songs improved and grew we decided we needed to do an album: *New Day Dawning* was launched after many months of hard work.

I could never have dreamed that God would use me to write lyrics and help produce an album of songs.

I want to encourage you. No matter how difficult your past, no matter what negative words have been spoken over your life, the Lord can turn things around. He is a God of the turnaround.

He is a God who can do extraordinary things, more than you could ever hope or imagine.

Now to him who is able to do immeasurably more than all we ask or imagine, according to his power that is at work within us …(Ephesians 3:20).

YOUNGER TALES

Sometimes your greatest fear can be one of your
greatest strengths.

16

Facing Clucky

I cowered in the corner of my playpen. On the other side, also cowering and staring straight back at me was Clucky, our bantam hen. We both stood there trembling, staring at each other, neither of us willing to move an inch.

How did I find myself in this position?

It had all started when Mum had gone off shopping for the afternoon and left me alone with Dad.

He had plans to get his garden planted and to keep me happy put me out on the terrace in my playpen.

After a while I got restless and started crying so Dad decided to let me out. Once free from the confines of the playpen I seized the moment to crawl excitedly into my father's newly-planted garden. As my father was hoeing and sowing I took great delight in eating dirt and pulling out some of the little cabbages. This was too much for Dad so he hatched another plan.

We had a bantam hen called Clucky; I was afraid of it. In desperation Dad placed me and Clucky together in my playpen. It worked a treat for two hours until Mum came home. When she saw Clucky and me together she was furious. Dad had some explaining to do.

Facing our fears

Forty years later I had to face Clucky again. One of my greatest fears has been public speaking. I have previously suffered from anxiety attacks, and was worried about losing my train of thought in public and making a fool of myself.

Our youth minister asked me to give a talk at the 6pm church service in a month's time. I accepted, but to minimise the possibility of getting stage fright I spent hours putting together a colourful PowerPoint presentation to distract the audience from looking at me. Every word for my presentation was written out. I would be able to read from notes, minimising the chance of having a blank mind and making a fool of myself.

Despite getting little sleep the night before, and having butterflies in my stomach, the presentation went down well. I even found there were parts of it I quite enjoyed. However, I did feel that my talk was too controlled and gave little freedom to utter any spontaneous thoughts.

Sometimes your greatest fear can be your greatest strength.

How I would have loved to be like other speakers - to be more at ease and able to speak 'off the cuff'!

As I did more and more public speaking I gained confidence. Now I am able to free myself from the burden of writing out every word and speak more freely. Today, when I tell people that I was once fearful of public speaking, they find it hard to believe. Some say, "You are such a natural." The fear has gone. In fact, I look forward to speaking.

Sometimes your greatest fear can be one of your greatest strengths. Because God is using me for his power and purposes I know he is going before me. I can hand every presentation over to him as I step up on the podium, in the knowledge that everything is for his glory. I'm no longer afraid. With God I can face any Clucky that comes along.

God did not give us a spirit of fear, but power, love and a sound mind (2 Timothy 1:7).

17

Lifting The Crust

I sensed another miracle in the waiting. It was my turn to cook and being a poor university student on a limited budget I had purchased some cheap stewing steak to serve up as my first effort.

It was our first week flatting and we had a meal roster in place. The four of us were scheduled to cook on either a Monday, Tuesday, Wednesday or Thursday.

Tuesday was my day and as I placed the cubes of meat inside the pressure cooker I marvelled at how these tough pieces of meat would be transformed into the most tender pieces in a matter of hours – the miracle of pressure cooking.

Six hours later, as I dished up the meat and carrot stew, one of my flatmates commented, "What are these black bits in the stew?"

I cheekily responded, "Mushrooms," knowing this was not true.

The stew was gobbled up and received some favourable reviews until it came time to clean up. As my flatmates placed the pressure cooker in the sink they discovered that the bottom of it was coated in an immovable black crust, hard as concrete. After many minutes of pointless hard scrubbing they had to have a rethink.

Frustrated, they decided to abandon this futile task and soak the crust in water overnight. The next morning as they revisited the pot the thick black crust had softened considerably and was easily removed.

This story reminds me of two powerful attributes of God: the process of refinement and of removing the crust.

The process of refinement

Before I became a Christian I had some tough parts in my heart, brought about by a feeling of inadequacy and low self-worth.

God has been able to take these hard parts and gradually soften and tenderise them. This is not something that can be done in a microwave, but through a slow but sure process of refinement.

He has also been using his power to refine me into his diamond. What I love about a diamond is that if you rub it in the dirt it is still a diamond, albeit a dirty one. You can throw a diamond down the toilet and as it emerges from the sewer pipe it still retains its value.

A diamond is so hard and almost impossible to dent or scratch as it has been subjected to so much pressure over thousands of years.

God can soften hard hearts.

Just as the pressure cooker worked its miracle on a cheap cut of meat God is working his miracle to tenderise my heart.

As you come to him, the living Stone — rejected by humans but chosen by God and precious to him (2 Peter 1:4).

Removing the crust

The second attribute of God is transformation, by soaking in him.

Just as the crust on the stew had to be soaked overnight to lose its hardness the stress and worry of living in the world takes its toll on us and sticks to us like mud.

We need something to lift the worries of the world off us. We can do this by soaking in the presence of God. It's very simple. Lie down, listen to worship music and focus on Jesus. Sometimes I may fall asleep during this process but I don't feel guilty.

When parenting, if one of my children fell asleep in my arms I would embrace it.

Lying in the arms of the Father in worship is an act of love and an act of surrender. When we are feeling anxious and stressed we can soak in the presence of God and find peace – soaking in the one who knows everything and is in complete control.

Bill Johnson, the senior leader of Bethel Church, California, says, "Since we always become like whatever we worship, there is nothing greater that God could want for his people than for them to worship him, for there is nothing greater than himself.

"God does not need our worship because he is some egotist in need of our affirmation. Instead, he longs for our transformation that takes place in the glory of his presence, the glory that descends in times of extended worship."[1]
As we soak in God's presence we are transformed to be more like Jesus. What could be better than being free and like Jesus?

> *Truly my soul finds rest in God;*
> *my salvation comes from him.*
> *Truly he is my rock and my salvation;*
> *he is my fortress, I will never be shaken.*
> *How long will you assault me?*
> *Would all of you throw me down—*
> *this leaning wall, this tottering fence?*
> *Surely they intend to topple me*
> *from my lofty place;*
> *they take delight in lies.*
> *With their mouths they bless,*
> *but in their hearts they curse.*
> *Yes, my soul, find rest in God;*
> *my hope comes from him.*
> (Psalm 62:1-5)

[1] Johnson, Bill Face to Face with God, Creation House, 2015

18

Tales Of The Unexpected

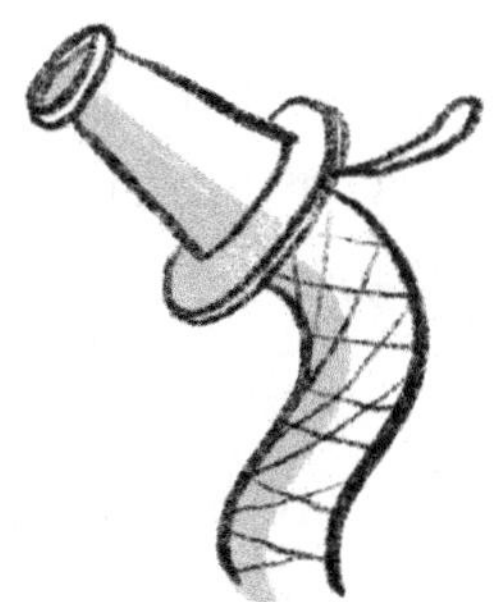

The temptation was too much. It was a hot summer's day at university. Sunbathing on the grass one floor below me were half a dozen engineering students.

For me, as a first-year accountancy student, they were easy bait. As I surveyed the scene from the first-floor common room I spied the fire hose in the corner and put my plan into action. I unreeled the hose slowly and surely towards the outside balcony. Once it was in position I turned it on. Screams, and some anger, issued from below.

"Let's get him!" they shouted.

I could hear students making a beeline for the stairwell. In haste I turned off the water and made a dash down the hallway to the safety of my room. As I cowered in my locked room

I could hear banging and shouting as the budding engineers tested the doors along the corridor.

Then something prompted me. It seemed so cowardly to hide in my room and not face up to my opponents. It was much more noble to step out and face them. Anyway, I was pretty sure none of them had spotted me. Facing up to them would be the last thing they would expect.

What was the worst that could happen? If they spotted me the most likely scenario was a dunking in the Avon River and it would all be over and done with in fifteen minutes. Or so I thought.

With a sense of fear and excitement I opened the door to my room and walked slowly out into the hallway. I heard someone shout from the far end of the hallway,

"It was him!"

At that moment I had three choices — either to run back into my room and lock the door or run for it down the other end of the hall way or pretend I didn't know what they were talking about. I chose the latter.

With some apprehension I started walking towards them.

As I drew near they stared at me, scanning my gangly, beanpole-like body and boyish, innocent-looking face. They started laughing, walked straight past me and continued banging loudly, continuing their search for the culprit.

I was not what they were expecting.

God of the unexpected

There are numerous examples in the Bible of the unexpected. Goliath was not expecting to be confronted and defeated by a boy shepherd named David, carrying only a sling and a stone.

So David triumphed over the Philistine with a sling and a stone; without a sword in his hand he struck down the Philistine and killed him (1 Samuel 17:50).

Gideon was not expecting God to tell him to reduce his army from twenty-two thousand to just three hundred to fight the Midianites.

The Lord said to Gideon, "With the three hundred men that lapped I will save you and give the Midianites into your hands. Let all the others go home (Judges 7:7).

When King Jehoshaphat of Judah marched out to confront the vast attacking armies of Ammon, Moab and Mount Seir with musical instruments and songs of praise, he did not expect the Lord to ambush these armies and completely destroy them, before he arrived on the battlefield.

As they began to sing and praise, the Lord set ambushes against the men of Ammon and Moab and Mount Seir who were invading Judah, and they were defeated.

The Ammonites and Moabites rose up against the men from Mount Seir to destroy and annihilate them. After they finished slaughtering the men from Seir, they helped to destroy one another.

When the men of Judah came to the place that overlooks the desert and looked toward the vast army, they saw only dead bodies lying on the ground; no one had escaped (2 Chronicles 20:22-24).

After being unsuccessful in lighting their altar the prophets of Baal were not expecting Elijah to pour large volumes of water over his bull sacrifice, before asking God to bring down his fire to light it.

Then the fire of the Lord fell and burned up the sacrifice, the wood, the stones and the soil, and also licked up the water in the trench (1 Kings 18:38).

The disciples did not expect Jesus to invite a crowd of five thousand to sit down and eat with them when they had barely enough food for themselves.

And he directed the people to sit down on the grass. Taking the five loaves and the two fish and looking up to heaven, he gave thanks and broke the loaves. Then he gave them to the disciples, and the disciples gave them to the people (Matthew 14:19).

The followers of Jesus did not expect their future King to ride into Jerusalem on a donkey.

The disciples went and did as Jesus had instructed them. They brought the donkey and the colt and placed their cloaks on them for Jesus to sit on (Matthew 21: 6-7).

And the Roman governor's soldiers mocked Jesus because he did not fit into their view of what a King of the Jews would look like.

Then they knelt in front of him and mocked him. "Hail, king of the Jews!" they said (Matthew 27:29).

These stories are a reminder that God does not do things our way and follow our rules. He is God.

With him anything is possible. With him we can defeat giants, win battles against the odds, multiply resources and turnaround any situation we are in.

God is in charge and will re-work things to our advantage and to his glory.

And it is also a reminder that God may be doing something in our lives or circumstances, totally different and much deeper than what we might expect.

19

Finding Your Sweet Spot

It was the annual university winter tournament and the Otago and Canterbury rugby league teams were playing each other. Otago found themselves two players short and the champion Canterbury team were keen for a more even contest.

I was at the tournament representing Canterbury University at table tennis. My friend Mark, who was the university rugby league hooker, asked me to help make up the numbers by playing for the Otago team. I had never played rugby league in my life but to help out a good mate I agreed.

Early in the game Mark received the ball. Seeing an opportunity to make an immediate impact I lined him up from ten metres away, lowered my shoulder and ran towards him, launching my 60kg lean frame like a scud missile to his hip region.

As my body crashed into him it was as though he had been hit by a ping-pong ball. I abruptly bounced off him and Mark continued to run freely, completely oblivious to my attempted tackle. I was left lying on the ground, dust in my mouth, clutching at thin air.

By the end of the game I doubt I made one effective tackle in our fifty-to-nil drubbing. I even had the ignominy of being dragged fifteen metres by a Canterbury player, as I held his legs, while he made his way to the try line.

I look back on that game and realise I was not built to play rugby league. I was made for less physical ball sports like table tennis and cricket.

David and Saul's armour

When David rose to the challenge of confronting the giant Goliath, King Saul asked David to try on his soldier's armour. David did but it didn't feel right, so he took it off.

Then Saul dressed David in his own tunic. He put a coat of armour on him and a bronze helmet on his head. David fastened on his sword over

*the tunic and tried walking around, because he was not used to them. "I
cannot go in these," he said to Saul, "because I am not used to them." So
he took them off* (1 Samuel 17:38-39).

As a young shepherd boy David was not used to carrying
heavy armour. He was accustomed to moving lightly, but he
was proficient with a sling and a stone.

The sling and stone was one of David's 'sweet spots'.

Everyone has a sweet spot

I believe that everyone is called to dream and was created with a
sweet spot, something unique and special that they are good at.

I wrote a song about this called *The Dreamer'*.

Here comes the dreamer the day dreamer
This is what he was born to do
Walking down a lonely road
His stories told as his life unfolds
Lift your eyes up from the ground
Bring your flavour and your sound
Anything alive is not just breathing
It's still dreaming of better days
You are a gift to the world
One of a kind, so don't be fooled
Lift your arms up to the sky
It will give you a reason why
Chorus
We all have a sweet spot
We were born to be

You're so special
You were born to be
Fly high in the sky

What is your dream? What are your sweet spots? Have you discovered something you are good at?

Releasing your greatness

Now here is a scary thought. How many people have taken their dreams to the grave – their art, music, engineering and poems?

Try not to be one of those. Your greatness is trapped in a seed within you. It will never die until you die. Don't give up on a God-given dream.

You are called to be fruitful. To release the dreams from the seeds planted within you. Be motivated to find the right people to encourage you to release your seeds.

Mark Twain said, "Keep away from people who try to belittle your ambitions. Small people always do that, but the really great make you feel that you, too, can become great."[2]

Create the right soil for these seeds to grow, nurture them and there will be fruit.

As my life journey unfolds I am discovering new things I can do that I never thought possible. The first forty years of my life were dominated by ball sports, but now I enjoy painting, song writing and writing.

If you are still searching for your sweet spots, remember God has created unique gifts in you, for his plans and purposes.

We have different gifts, according to the grace given to each of us. If your gift is prophesying, then prophesy in accordance with your faith; if it is serving, then serve; if it is teaching, then teach; if it is to encourage, then give encouragement; if it is giving, then give generously; if it is to lead, do it diligently; if it is to show mercy, do it cheerfully (Romans 12:6-8).

» [1] https://open.spotify.com/track/3sw0xqZ9V6JWD5PhwTNtqT
» [1] https://robwhelanmusic.bandcamp.com/track/the-dreamer
» [2] www.goodreads.com

GRACE AND TRUTH

God looks at beauty within the heart.

20

The Age Of Scepticism

Before the internet came along we would find answers to our questions through someone wise we trusted. It may have been our parents, grandparents, teacher, neighbour or someone else we thought was wise.

We would firmly believe what they told us. Their word was taken for granted.

One of the best pieces of advice I ever received was from my father. At the young age of twenty-three I found myself managing a team of twenty. My father said to me, "If you can keep seventy-five percent of your staff happy seventy-five percent of the time you are doing well."

This taught me not to try and please everybody. I realised there would always be people who did not agree with my ideas. If I tried to please everybody things would end up in chaos, with no-one happy.

My father's wise words stuck with me, and five years later I found myself successfully managing a team of forty-eight.

Dad was always there in other areas of my life too – when I needed a loan, a babysitter or help with house repairs or landscaping. He was someone I could always rely upon.

Today, the word of mouth is one of the last things we rely upon. Even the written word is seen as second rate compared to what is available online.

A rich source of information?

The internet is perceived as a rich source of information. Often it is our first point of reference. Thanks to internet search engines it is easy to find answers to any question.

However, there are now so many competing voices on the internet that it is difficult to discern what is the most accurate answer.

Search engine algorithms will even give you the answer you want, to validate your point of world view.

This can lead to entrenched views, confusion, information overload and scepticism. To counter this, some media organisations now take pride in their 'fact checking' of information. But even 'fact checking' is subject to question, because it can be manipulated to favour one side of an argument.

To add to the confusion, foreign governments are now being implicated in plots to influence peoples' opinions by spreading false information. It is becoming more and more difficult to determine what is accurate.

What are the facts? What is the unbiased truth?

One book is rock solid

While this turmoil is spreading around us there is one source of information that remains rock solid. It has been in print for many hundreds of years yet still remains as relevant today as it was one hundred years ago. It even contains a warning that we are not to manipulate or change its text.

And if anyone takes words away from this scroll of prophecy, God will take away from that person any share in the tree of life and in the Holy City, which are described in this scroll (Revelation 22:19).

It is called the Bible, the living word of God. Every time you read it you can gain a new perspective. It speaks into a situation in your life today and tomorrow. It's a book that is ageless, timeless, prophetic and lifegiving.

Many times I have looked for a word of encouragement and comfort, and found a passage that was just what I needed for that day.

Recently I was meditating on Psalm 16 in the Passion Translation and came across this passage that resonated with me:

Your pleasant path leads me to pleasant places.
I'm overwhelmed by the privileges
That come from following you,
For you have given me the best!
The way you counsel and correct me makes me praise you more,
For your whispers in the night give me wisdom,
Showing me what to do next (Psalm 16:6-7).

I was particularly struck by the words 'your whispers in the night' as often the Lord has awakened me in the middle of the night to reveal something.

It may be a word of knowledge about a problem I am facing or it could be a call to prayer.

Christchurch earthquake 2010

One of the more dramatic examples of this happened a few years ago.

I was asleep in Wellington on the morning of the 4th September 2010 and remember being woken up at 4.35 am to this voice saying, "Pray for the children of Christchurch."

Fifteen minutes later I turned on the radio and discovered that a 7.1 magnitude earthquake had struck Darfield near Christchurch. As it turned out, only one person died as a direct result of that first earthquake and few people were injured.

I had no inkling that there would be a second, far more tragic one, a few months later.

Alive and active

There are 150 Psalms in the Bible. Someone once said to me that whatever you are facing in life God has a Psalm for you for each day.

For a couple of years I suffered from a lack of sleep. It would take me hours to get to sleep but I would wake up after another few hours and struggle to get back.

When I told my friend Mary about this problem she told me that she had also suffered from not sleeping, but a friend of hers had given her a verse (Psalm 4:8) that helped her immensely. After praying this verse each night, it had remedied her sleep problem.

In peace I will lie down and sleep, for you alone, Lord, make me dwell in safety (Psalm 4:8)

So, from that moment I prayed this verse every night when I went to bed. Within a week I was sleeping soundly every night, and still do so.

I had tried sleep programmes and the occasional sleeping pill, but this verse was the answer. It laid my sleeping problem to rest.

Not only can we trust the authenticity of the Bible, but it is alive and active and a huge source of comfort in a world in desperate need of hope.

For the word of God is alive and active. Sharper than any double-edged sword, it penetrates even to dividing soul and spirit, joints and marrow; it judges the thoughts and attitudes of the heart (Hebrews 4:12).

21

Being A Truth Teller

One of the first stories we published in the Daily Encourager was about a woman from Porirua, New Zealand, Maarametua Williams.

For years she had been a methamphetamine (P) addict but had recently turned her life around. At the time of the interview she had been off the drug for eighteen months and was helping others leave P behind.

Maarametua frankly described what P will do to you, and all it takes is one puff.

You will lose your dignity, family, friends, job, happiness, mind and pride. You will rob, steal, cheat, lie and beg. You will end up with no money, alone, homeless, in prison or dead.

I admired her directness and determination to help others and leave this terrible addiction behind.

Maarametua Williams is a truth teller. She tells it like it is and does not hold back.

It got me thinking. As Christians how far are we prepared to go to stand for the truth?

The confrontation

A couple of years ago I was in Christchurch in Cathedral Square. A man was expounding the Word of God to a small crowd.

How far are we prepared to go for the truth?

There was another man sitting nearby, dressed in a black jacket and wearing dark glasses, contradicting every word the speaker said.

As the evangelist spoke this man would shout out something like, "That's not right. That's a bunch of fairy tales. Only an idiot would believe this God nonsense."

As I listened to this confrontation I felt God calling me to sit next to this man, even though he looked a little bit intimidating. I asked, "What do you think of the preaching?"

"It's just a load of old nonsense, isn't it?" he responded.

I mentioned that he seemed like a nice person who cared about people. He agreed.

"Yes, I am a nice person and I do care about people."

I told him I used to think God was a load of nonsense too, but that all changed when he did a miracle healing on my foot. I now believe God is real and even speaks to us.

After listening to me talking about God for a short time his retort was swift and curt. "Well, how does God speak to you? In Arabic, or is it in Japanese?"

I laughed.

"Sometimes," I said, "it's just an impression and not necessarily an audible voice."

I was not brave enough to tell him God had told me to sit next to him. Anyway, we chatted further for a short time and I wished him all the best. Then I asked him if I could bless him before I went on my way.

He said he did not want a blessing, but I blessed him anyway and shook his hand on friendly terms as I left.

I wondered afterwards what the purpose was of my engagement with this man. It certainly quietened him down while the speaker was talking to the crowd.

Something deeper

But was there something deeper present?

I had come to him and told him that God was real and that I could see he was a nice person. I had shared my healing testimony with him. Only God knows the impact of our conversation.

I would like to think that it softened the man's heart. Perhaps he is still reflecting on our conversation? Perhaps he is starting to have doubts about his own beliefs? Perhaps he is listening more to what the evangelist is saying and interrupting less?

All I know is that I was given an opportunity to speak up, in truth.

I was not prepared to let lies undermine what the evangelist was saying, and tried to confront this out of love, not because I am particularly brave, but because I felt God's hand leading me to speak the truth.

For the law was given through Moses; grace and truth came through Jesus Christ (John 1:17).

22

Half An Egg

Half a rasher of bacon and half an egg were the breakfast rations at a Westport boarding house where my father lived in the early 1950s, just after the Second World War, when food rationing was in place in New Zealand.

The egg was fried 'sunny side up' so it could easily be cut in half. To fill their stomachs the boarders would eat the half portions with lots of bread, as bread was not rationed.

As my father told me this story it got me thinking about halves, particularly about moments when I have hastily jumped to a conclusion on a matter, or judged someone from their looks without knowing much about the person.

Knowing all the facts

I wonder how many times I have listened to someone, or read something in the newspaper or online, but only gained half the story. Or, I wonder how often I have had a complete account of a situation and known the unequivocal balanced truth.

Rarely would I have been in this situation. It is most likely when I have experienced something first-hand. Even then, a personal experience can be open to your own interpretation.

There are many obstacles to getting a complete understanding of a situation. Maybe a person describing a situation puts his own slant on it, or maybe we only hear what we want to hear or read what we want to read.

As I grow older I have learnt that there are always two sides to a story. Wisdom teaches that it is better to take time to pause, weigh up, seek the counsel of others and sift the facts.

For lack of guidance a nation falls, but victory is won through many advisers (Proverbs 11:14).

Life can be complicated and there are not always easy answers. If someone is passionate about something and their passion causes them to speak or write in a slightly biased way it is still well worth exploring the reasons behind their belief. A gem of understanding might be realised, a gem you might have missed if you had rushed for judgement.

It is wise to take time to weigh up and sift the facts.

I remember once being in a deep discussion with one of my daughters about abortion. I am conservative and she is more liberal in her thinking. Her views completely opened up my mind to things I had never considered and made me realise how complex this issue is. My overall view did not change but it gave me a much greater appreciation of the situation.

Judging a book by its cover

A few years ago, once a month, my church prayer team used to visit a group of people for a potluck dinner at a church in Wellington.

We would give testimony and pray for them after dinner. Many of these people looked different. Some were obese and some quite eccentric. It didn't take me long to judge them and I found it was awkward to converse with them.

But there was one man who intrigued me. He wore shabby clothes, his sole form of transport was an old bike, and he would eat some strange-looking food from a jar, instead of sharing food with us from the table.

One day I made an effort to engage with him, thinking I might be able to help him. I asked him why he ate his food from a jar. He told me that his sole mission in life was to sacrifice food, clothing and other good things so he could fund Bibles in China. He lived a very frugal life, saving every cent, so he could make a maximum impact spreading the gospel in China.

I was immediately convicted.

I thought I might have been able to help him when, in actual fact, he made me seriously think about how much I was sacrificing in my own life for God.

There was also a lady there who was badly overweight and had mobility problems. I made a special effort to talk to her and when I did the words that flowed from her lips reflected a beautiful love of God; they were quite profound.

This made me question the depth of my relationship with God.

What does God think?

While the world judges things by outward appearance God has another definition of what 'beautiful' looks like. He looks at beauty within the heart.

God doesn't want us to rush to judgement. We should not believe everything we hear or read, without

God looks at beauty within the heart.

question. We must use our own discernment.

Jessie Penne-Lewis in her classic book *War on the Saints* talks about the dangers of being passive and not thinking things through thoroughly.

She says, "Rather than us being a passive slave, God requires us to co-operate with him fully, through His Spirit, and act intelligently."

Do not conform to the pattern of this world, but be transformed by the renewing of your mind. Then you will be able to test and approve what God's will is – his good, pleasing and perfect will (Romans 12:2).

I am slowly learning not to judge people by their appearance, to hold my tongue and not quickly jump to conclusions. I need to use my own discernment in co-operation with the Holy Spirit to seek out a fuller understanding and truth.

We must not become robotic in our thoughts. Bill Johnson describes this rather eloquently: "We are not designed to be robots. We are planted in a kingdom and invited to explore."

By not judging a person from their looks or rushing to a conclusion on a matter we could avoid 'having egg on our face'.

23

Quiet Grace

I have been in many situations where I have felt guilt and shame and wondered whether they could ever be turned around for good.

At work once my boss was fuming, not at me personally, but at my department and in particular at one of my staff members who had made a serious error of judgement. It was his right to direct his anger at me as I was responsible for the overall running of the department.

I felt terrible that I had let him down. He was someone I truly respected. And I knew it was my job to see the issue was dealt with and prevented from happening again. That afternoon I set about to do so. I wondered if the good relationship I had built up with him over a decade would ever be the same again.

The next day, and after a sleepless night, I found out. I unexpectedly met him in the lift. He smiled and wished me a good day. It was as if nothing had happened. Yesterday's problem seemed forgotten and didn't define the day or the next. Perhaps the reputation I had built up over the past ten years had protected me?

I was convicted but not condemned. I was free to move on. It felt like a quiet grace.

Northern Ireland

My protestant family hailed from Northern Ireland where we had been at war with the Catholics for decades. One of my family members was shot dead in cold blood by the IRA and this festered within the family for many years.

He was a university lecturer. It was believed the Catholics wanted to take control of the places of learning, replacing him with a Catholic lecturer to fulfil their objectives.

Amazing act of grace

However, after decades of fighting and many killings one act of grace changed everything.

In 1987 an IRA bomb exploded in a small town west of Belfast amongst a group of Protestants who had gathered to honour the war-dead on veterans' day.

Eleven people died and sixty-three were wounded. What made this act of terrorism stand out from so many others was the response of one of the wounded, Gordon Wilson, a devout Methodist. The bomb buried Wilson and his twenty-year-old daughter, Marie, under five feet of concrete and rubble.

"Daddy, I love you very much," were the last words Marie spoke, grasping her father's hand as they waited for the rescuers. She suffered severe spinal and brain injuries and died a few hours later in the hospital.

A newspaper later proclaimed that no one remembered what the politicians had to say at the time. No one who heard Gordon Wilson will ever forget what he confessed. His grace towered over the miserable justifications of the bombers.

Speaking from his hospital bed, Wilson said: "I have lost my daughter but I bear no grudge. Bitter talk is not going to bring Marie Wilson back to life. I shall pray tonight and every night that God will forgive them."[1]

His daughter's last words were words of love and Gordon Wilson was determined to live out his life on that plane of love.

"The World Wept," said one report, as Wilson gave a similar interview on BBC radio that week.

A world of increasing division

Today, it seems like we live in a world displaying little grace, a world that is becoming increasingly divided, with people being pigeon-holed into groups of like-minded people.

Which group do you belong to? For the vaccine or anti-vax? Right wing or left wing? In favour of abortion or pro-life? For gender fluidity or are you homophobic? Do Black Lives Matter or all lives?

Your choice determines the box you are put into.

Unfortunately, within this stereotyping there is a complete lack of grace. There is little room for listening, compassion, understanding and love. Everything can look black or white when in reality there are various shades of grey.

I wonder how long this will continue. Can Christians douse the flames of division? Can we anchor ourselves in a different world, one full of compassion, understanding and grace? The devil wants to sow division and confusion, but we are called to be peacemakers.

In Matthew 8: 23-27 Jesus was in a boat with his disciples, sleeping, when a furious storm arose. The disciples were afraid they were going to drown but Jesus rebuked the winds and waves, and it became completely calm. He was able to calm the storm because the peace that was 'within him' was greater than the storm 'around him'.

May we as Christians know the peace and grace of God so deeply that we are able to calm the storms around us and bring peace and hope to a troubled world.

It could be quite simple. When someone is expressing a contrary view we could learn to listen more, talk less, build empathy and

We are called to be peacemakers.

express love in a way that does not compromise our beliefs. Because we have an understanding of God' grace and unconditional love for us we can let this flow out in grace and love to others.

For if, by the trespass of the one man, death reigned through that one man, how much more will those who receive God's abundant provision of grace and of the gift of righteousness reign in life through the one man, Jesus Christ! (Romans 5:17)

»   [1] *What's So Amazing About Grace*, Phillip Yancey

FINAL REFLECTIONS

When we leave this planet the most powerful thing
we leave here are our stories.

24

Looking Beyond The Box

Gold dust was raining down from the ceiling. As the tiny flakes floated in the air mass hysteria broke out across the room. Hundreds of people were screaming with excitement, chasing after the flakes of gold.

As I watched in awe there suddenly appeared tiny feathers fluttering past my face. This was new and different; feathers so small and yet so exquisite.

I thought to myself, *this could only have come from God.*

This was the second Sunday in a row that Bethel Church in Redding, California, had experienced the glory cloud of God. And I was there, to witness this in person. It had been an amazing week. I had also witnessed many other miracles.

On a previous trip to Bethel Church a man had prayed for my leg to grow longer. This was to fix a problem I had with one leg being shorter than the other. I saw it lengthen before me and my reaction at the time was to break out in astonished laughter.

After the gold dust and feathers experience I once again returned to New Zealand with amazing stories. I was, however, puffed up with pride about the miracles I had seen God do. I believed I was moving in a much higher place than some of the other more conservative members of my church. They didn't seem to get it. I thought they were too blinkered in their thinking.

You can't put God in a box

A few weeks later I couldn't attend the usual 10.30 am morning service and went along to the 9.00 am one instead. This was our more traditional service with no electric guitars or drums, where they played the organ and sang hymns. I decided to grin and bear it.

Part-way through the service the minister read from the 1662 Anglican Prayer Book. The most beautiful words flowed from his lips, words that had been wonderfully constructed. They demonstrated an amazing love and faith in God. I was mesmerized; it didn't take long for tears to fill my eyes.

I wondered how something written 400 years ago could be so relevant and inspiring today, and I was immediately convicted.

How could I, a Christian of fewer than five years, think I knew it all? Who was I to judge these so-called conservative

Christians? I realised that I had been putting God in a box and I needed to open my mind.

They shall not grow old

On the same theme of opening our minds, a couple of years ago I watched the Peter Jackson's World War 1 movie *They Shall Not Grow Old*. This is a very moving tribute, based on historical footage, to what the young soldiers endured during the war.

Little did I know that when these soldiers returned home after the war many found it difficult to get a job. Sadly, what they had been through was unappreciated and forgotten. I was deeply impacted, and it made me appreciate what my grandfather and others sacrificed and suffered for the love of their country.

Similarly, my late father recounted that during depression years of the 1930s his parents would, as a treat, prepare a meal of mutton flap soup for themselves and their four children. The children would get to eat the flakes of meat and their parents would drink the soup water as their meal.

He told me how the family only had one pair of shoes each and these were for church. They went to school in bare feet, even in the Christchurch winter. Dad said their feet hardened and it didn't take long for the frostbite to heal.

It is so easy to forget the sacrifices that have gone before us. It is so easy to box up our thoughts and think we know the answers, when there is so much more to be revealed.

From now on I want to make a special effort to appreciate our past and value people better. We have a lot to learn from history and everyone has a story and something to teach us. Let us not judge and have preconceived ideas, but open our eyes with empathy.

I love how Mark Twain summed this up: "When I was a boy of fourteen my father was so ignorant I could hardly stand to have the old man around. But when I got to be twenty-one I was astonished at how much the old man had learned in seven years." [1]

Children, obey your parents in the Lord, for this is right. Honour your father and mother. This is the first commandment with a promise; so that it may go well with you and that you may enjoy long life on the earth (Ephesians 6:1-3.)

[1] www.goodreads.com

25

Embracing Our Flavours

The city of Wellington is blessed with a variety of restaurants that add to the flavour of the city – Indian, Thai, Moroccan, Cambodian, Mongolian, Greek, Malaysian, Italian, Mexican, Vietnamese, Irish, Chinese, Middle Eastern, Japanese and French. Take your pick.

Wellington is a much richer place due to the diversity of its restaurants and cultures. In the same way, I think the All Blacks are a much better team because of the different skillsets and talents Māori and Pacific Islanders bring to the team.

My life has certainly been enriched from travelling overseas and associating with people from different cultures – in North and Central America, the United Kingdom, Western Europe, Turkey, Morocco, Uganda, South Africa, China, India,

Cambodia, Japan, the Pacific Islands and Australia.

In the vast majority of those countries I was warmly received as a New Zealander. I felt honoured and respected and there was a sense of flavour in those relationships.

My eyes were opened to different ways of life. It made me realise how fortunate I am to live in New Zealand. Whenever I return here the grass seems greener, the leaves more vibrant, the air cleaner, the water purer, and there is a lot more space to enjoy our country's natural beauty.

Experiencing other cultures with my children

When my children turned eighteen years old I decided to treat each one of them to an overseas trip for their birthdays. This was a way for them to spend one-on-one time with their dad as well as experiencing different cultures.

When my eldest daughter turned eighteen I told her I had bought her something very special for her birthday. She looked at me excitedly and asked if it was a car.

"No," I responded. "I have bought you something much better – an overseas trip."

"That's great," she said, "Are we going to Europe?"

"No. I'm taking you to India for three weeks," I replied.

Her face dropped, but over the next few months she became increasingly excited about the prospect. During those three weeks in India we experienced many highs and lows. I know the experience opened her eyes to a whole new way of life. It helped her appreciate both how others live and the value of what she has. She has since pursued a successful career in the travel business.

Learning from other cultures

Over the past three years I have had the honour of attending two hui. These were quite emotional events where there was a deep reconciliation between Pakeha and Māori. I will never forget the love and forgiveness displayed by my Māori colleagues. I began to see Māori culture in a new light, especially the importance they place on people and environmental sustainability.

A visit to Tonga a few years ago also changed my perception about how to honour and respect people. It was my friend's birthday and was being held at his father's home in Nuku'alofa. Around thirty people were present and there was an abundance of food. Before we sat down to eat we all gathered in the main living room, sitting on the floor. My friend thanked us for coming to his birthday.

He then went around the room and told each one of us gracefully what we meant to him. There were tears as he shared his thoughts. We all felt truly honoured and made to feel special in the parts we had played in his life.

After he had finished speaking we all got a chance to let him know about how special he was to us. There was humour and more tears as we all bonded in one big family. The occasion demonstrated to me the respect Tongan people have for their families and friends, and why they're so close.

Helping each other as a family

Just as every culture is unique and has different flavours the families we belong to have different flavours, which can create challenges.

Each family member has a unique personality, skin colour, varying moods, ways of dressing and points of view. We get on better with some members of the family than with others.

Most cultures emphasise 'family' strongly.

Keeping family close requires a commitment of time, an ability to listen, a little empathy and sometimes forgiveness and grace. There are rewards that accrue from an investment in family and learning from its members.

Most cultures, despite their differences, place a strong emphasis on family. This might express itself differently from what you might find in traditional western culture, brought home to me after a discussion with an Indian friend.

He was the middle of three boys in his family. The youngest brother found the love of his life and got married first. He wanted to buy a house for his new wife but, being the younger brother, he needed a large mortgage to fund the purchase. So, the two other brothers helped with the deposit and sacrificially saved to help their younger brother pay off the mortgage quickly.

This type of scenario would have played itself out in families across many different cultures. Can you think of members of your family who made a sacrifice to build a generational legacy?

Fusion cooking

In cooking there is a term called 'fusion', where you take the best ingredients from different regions and combine them. Fusion food has become popular because it offers culinary adventures based on unique and distinctive tastes, bringing more colour to culinary culture.

Perhaps we can take a lesson from fusion cooking? Combine the best ingredients from different cultures to create a better society. However, there will always be ingredients in different cultures that will be difficult to mix. One of these is religion.

Some people believe that all religions are the same or that the world would be a much better place if we got rid of religion. Everyone is entitled to his or her belief, but this has not been my experience. Out of all the ingredients in the world's main religions there is one key ingredient – Jesus.

Like salt, Jesus adds flavour and acts as a preservative. He holds all things together and is the source of all I need. He is before all things, and in him all things hold together (Colossians 1:17).

It is Christ in me which makes me valuable, gives me flavour and is the one ingredient I cannot water down. *Christ in you, the hope or glory* (Colossians 1:27).

26

Born Good

A few years ago I spent a week visiting a prison on a church outreach. We would arrive as a team early in the morning to witness to prisoners at Rimutaka Prison. They had expressed an interest in learning more about Jesus.

I discovered faces that were covered in shame and torn by guilt, but when I engaged with them, one by one, and expressed a genuine interest in them their faces would light up. They really wanted to change and do good.

It makes me wonder whether goodness is born within all of us, waiting for the right moment.

Christchurch

I have been very encouraged by the heart-warming stories of how the people of the beleaguered city of Christchurch have responded positively to a series of tragedies.

In the face of devastation from earthquakes and a mass shooting people stepped up to display sacrificial love, generosity and kindness. Tragedy brought out the best in humanity.

It was very humbling to witness the local Muslim response to the mass shooting, that was filled with grace, forgiveness and love.

Is goodness born within us?

The movie world often paints a dim, apocalyptic view of a world short on resources, tainted with greed, violence and lust. In Christchurch the opposite became true. In the wake of catastrophe the community reached out and racial divisions melted away. Neighbours got to know each other better, many performing acts of kindness and sharing resources.

It got me thinking. Why did these tragedies bring out the best in the people of Christchurch? Is goodness instinctive, or was this response unique to Christchurch?

Wellington's shining example

In Wellington I have seen another example of inherent goodness. His name is Daniel. Daniel is often seen sitting outside a shop in central Wellington. He has overcome much hardship and disappointment in his life. As a child he nearly died, twice. A traumatic motorbike accident fractured his spine in three places causing constant on-going pain and putting most jobs beyond his reach. If it wasn't for the prayer he received he probably wouldn't be alive today.

Daniel has also suffered the loss of close members of his family and the murder of a homeless acquaintance. He has fought depression, emotional and physical pain, and has suffered verbal abuse from passers-by who have not stopped to hear his story, many presuming he is on drugs.

In spite of this, Daniel has a cheery word to say to everyone. He returns good for evil. When abuse comes his way he gives a blessing, he empathises with others in adverse circumstances and has a true heart of compassion. This man has a purpose in life.

He has been on the streets for over five years and met hundreds of people. He says, "I've talked to Japanese, Muslims, English,

Asians, Africans and many cultures and backgrounds and found good in them all."

Many well-wishers give him food. Yet, if he has anything in excess of his own needs he gives it away to others in need.

Daniel has a gentle spirit, a generous heart and a genuine desire to bestow blessing and love on everyone who passes by him, regardless of their attitudes toward him. He may not realise that to those of us who have stopped to hear his story and bless him he is, in turn, a blessing to us. In fact, if he was not seen on the streets of Wellington for a period of time many people would be concerned for his wellbeing.

We can be greatly encouraged by Daniel, knowing what he has suffered and still suffers on a daily basis – pain, abuse, being misunderstood and rejected. Yet, seeing him give out to others with such love and compassion inspires me to do the same. I am not sure if Daniel has a faith, but kindness, generosity and love naturally flow from him.

Hope for mankind

The three examples, above - prison, Christchurch and Daniel - give hope for humankind.

Genesis 1:27 says: *So God created mankind in his own image, in the image of God he created them; male and female he created them.*

God saw all that he had made, and it was very good (Genesis 1:31).

Before sin came into the world everything God made was good.

Letting goodness flow

Before I became a Christian I did good things. There was goodness in me. However, that flow of goodness was limited by my belief system. When I found Jesus I realised that I didn't have to compare myself to others. I was in a godly kingdom where the resources were infinite and there was no need for jealousy. Goodness could flow whatever the cost.

As a Christian I believe we have a mandate not only to demonstrate goodness but also to bring out the best in others. This doesn't need to be complicated. It can simply be valuing and listening to people and helping them with something they are not good at. We need to demonstrate love at the coalface to show God's love and value for every person.

Act of kindness

It could be a small act of kindness.

A number of years ago I moved to a neighbourhood where a large Chinese family lived next door to me. For the first year I had little to do with them. One day I did a small act of kindness for them. This brought a smile to their faces and opened a door. Suddenly I was treated to exceptional hospitality and would be given food or invited over for large family gatherings. Fear gave way to love.

An encouraging word

I love meeting new people from all countries and all walks of life. I enjoy asking them: "What are you passionate about?" I try to encourage them.

I often wonder what happens after you have given someone an encouraging word. How did it impact them or change the direction of their life in a positive way?

Sometimes, somebody I haven't seen for years will remind me how I once encouraged them with a word. Nothing brings me greater joy.

An encouraging word breaks down barriers and builds people up.

Do not let any unwholesome talk come out of your mouths, but only what is helpful for building others up according to their needs, that it may benefit those who listen (Ephesians 4:29).

27

Now Is The Time To Sing

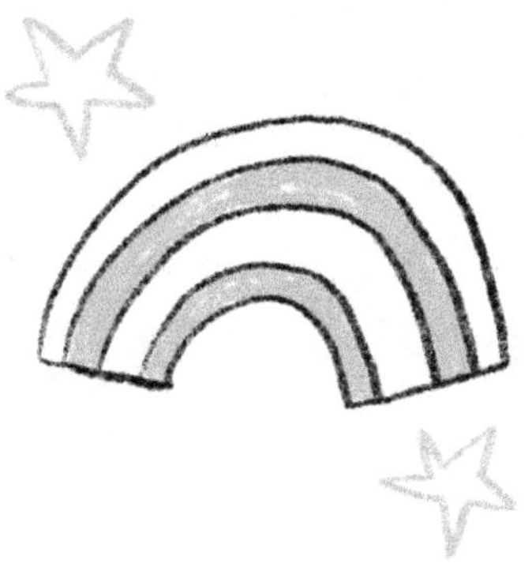

The world today seems to be full of fear. We are inundated with negative news and people are desperate for hope. Every day we hear about bad things happening. In 2020/21 we faced the coronavirus pandemic, loss of jobs and climate change.

People's lives and livelihoods were at stake as we moved into unchartered territory. To counter these events we were forced to adopt severe measures.

Lockdowns seem to come and go. Schools and universities have been closed for periods of time. Conferences, sporting events and concerts have been deferred or cancelled. Major travel restrictions were in place globally.

We were told not to shake hands with people, not to go to work if we have a runny nose and avoid crowded areas if we are over 60 or have health problems.

These restrictions were unprecedented in our generation. One needs to go back over 100 years to the Spanish flu of 1918 to find similar restrictions in place.

We were asked to self-isolate for a fourteen-day period if we thought we had come in contact with somebody who had tested positive for the coronavirus.

I remember the stress of being in my first lockdown. Here's the diary of my first day.

Lockdown diary

I need to go to the supermarket. I'm out of some basic necessities and need to stock up.

After arriving at New World I wait in the line outside. There are white markers to keep people apart. Every few minutes a lady dressed in black, wearing a white mask and gloves, calls us in three at a time. It is surreal.

Checkout operators stand behind Perspex shields and frantically spray the surfaces with sanitiser. I have to take my purchases and bag them myself. The operator is not allowed to touch my shopping bags. Once I get home I'm still feeling unnerved by the experience. Have I brought home the virus? What is it attached to?

I wash my hands and place a plastic bag of apples and paper towels on the bench. I decide to leave them there for 48 hours. I figure after that period of time the virus will get bored and eat itself.

I've also brought home some baked goods – Danish pastries and muffins. They were really cheap and I could not resist a bargain. People are obviously worried about buying them but I have a plan. I put them in the freezer. I'm aware that the coronavirus has not touched Antarctica.

Time for lunch. I over-boil some soup and sit down with a piece of toast. I'm still worried about my hands being contaminated so I stab the piece of toast with a fork and eat it from the fork. I think that's a smart thing to do. Later, I realise I took the piece of toast out of the toaster with my bare hands.

After lunch it's raining and I would love to venture outside. A friend of mine living in a small apartment in Wellington feels the same way. She messages through a picture with the caption: 'Feeding the ducks'.

I'm tired of being indoors and since it is only drizzling I put on my raincoat and venture out. As I walk down the road the sun comes out and a beautiful rainbow forms over Wellington harbour. I feel this is a promise. Things are going to be okay.

Suddenly, dozens of people line the streets – families, couples, singles. The streets are filled with people. I walk past one lady and she complains I am walking around her block anti-clockwise. It's good that people have not lost their sense of humour.

So many people are out walking and enjoying the experience. I've re-learned how to sidestep so I am out of harm's way whenever I encounter another human. I run into some people I've not seen for a couple of months. We stop and chat from a strict two-metre distance. The chat is very casual. I walk past the tennis club. How I long to play tennis again with my tennis mates. Once I arrive home I chat with my bubble next door. She has been for a walk too.

My daughter in Christchurch texts through a picture of my new grandson. I'm so proud of him sitting up. How I long to hold him. How I long for my family and friends.

Where our hope is

This turmoil and upheaval in the world provides a wonderful opportunity for Christians to stand out and showcase their joy and faith in the Lord.

As I was writing this I felt the Lord say, "Now is the time to sing. Do not put your hope in a cure for the coronavirus. Do not put your hope in the share market recovering. Do not put your hope in worldly possessions. Your hope is in the Lord."

Then I saw a picture of a large cruise ship laden with people. Everyone on board was singing with joy. Because they were singing in unity the ship was able to sail through rough waters unhindered.

I interpret the picture to mean the Lord saying that now is the time for the church to be unified and joyful. Now is the time for us to stand up and display the fruits of the Spirit.

But the fruit of the Spirit is love, joy, peace, forbearance, kindness, goodness, faithfulness, gentleness and self-control. Against such things there is no law (Galatians 5:22-23).

Now is not the time for us to be fearful.

For the Spirit God gave us does not make us timid, but gives us power, love and self-discipline (2 Timothy 1:7).

We do not need to be frightened. We are called to shine when faced with insurmountable problems in a dark world.

I know of situations where nonbelievers have approached Christians because they stand out. There is something about them that is attractive, that the non-believers don't have. It is easy to get caught up in the panic of the world.

I take particular comfort from Psalm 112.

Praise the Lord.
Blessed are those who fear the Lord,
who find great delight in his commands.
Their children will be mighty in the land;
the generation of the upright will be blessed.
Wealth and riches are in their houses,
and their righteousness endures forever.
Even in darkness light dawns for the upright,
for those who are gracious and compassionate and righteous.
Good will come to those who are generous and lend freely,
who conduct their affairs with justice.
Surely the righteous will never be shaken;
they will be remembered forever.
They will have no fear of bad news;
their hearts are steadfast, trusting in the Lord.
Their hearts are secure, they will have no fear;
in the end they will look in triumph on their foes.
They have freely scattered their gifts to the poor,
their righteousness endures forever;
their horn will be lifted high in honour. The wicked will see and be
vexed,

> *they will gnash their teeth and waste away;*
> *the longings of the wicked will come to nothing.*

Let us stand out for our love, joy, peace, patience, kindness, goodness, faithfulness, gentleness and self-control. Let us stand up unified as a church. This is a time for us to shine and sing, and watch the Lord bring in a harvest.

28

What Is Your Legacy?

How do you want to be commemorated? How do you want your children, friends and family to remember you? What impact will your life have had on them?

Late in her life I gave my eighty-six-year-old mother a book to complete. It was called *Grandma, Tell Me Your Story*. It was a chance for her to share her stories and answer questions about the best memories of her life. A couple of months later she passed away.

It was sudden, but she was at peace as she held the hand of her husband of sixty-three years and closed her eyes.

At her funeral we sent her off in a bright-red coffin to the sound of Coronation Street, a programme she adored. She leaves a legacy for her children, grandchildren and great grandchildren.

The book is an absolute treasure, filled with wisdom, honesty and happy memories in words and pictures. It took her a month to complete before she passed away.

Never a dull moment

My mum had a sense of humour.

For Mum and Dad's first date they decided to go the movies. Mum agreed to buy the tickets as Dad was on night shift. As they were driving to the theatre she told him she had had a problem purchasing the tickets. She hadn't been able to get two tickets seated together. It wasn't all bad news though, as she had managed to get them seated either side of the aisle. They would still be able to see each other.

Dad started thinking that this was one of the dumbest women he had ever dated. The date was going to be a complete waste of time.

When they arrived at the theatre, to his surprise, they were actually seated together. Dad realised that this woman was made of sterner stuff than he initially thought. Later, Mum admitted she was testing him. He had passed.

After sixty-three years of marriage, Mum said to Dad on her deathbed, "I have to tell you something. Those fawn trousers, those ratty ones that you use for gardening, I've hidden them. You will never find them."

Dad went mad and said, "I need them and I want them. It doesn't matter if the hems are frayed because the hems are hidden inside my gumboots."

Mum said, "I'm not going to tell you where they are. I will tell Lynne (daughter)."

Then, before she had time to tell Lynne, she closed her eyes and went to sleep.

Mum was also a battler. For nearly fifty years she suffered from the pain and disfigurement of rheumatoid arthritis, but this didn't stop her. She always kept herself busy.

In her book *Grandma Tell Me Your Story* she answers the prompting questions with blunt authenticity.

Grandma, what was your mom like? Can you tell a story that describes her personality or values?

My mum was a very talented lady all her life, she learnt to carve when she was 17yrs old & made some amazing pieces of furniture a piano stool, a folding fire screen 7 pieces all together. she was a good pianist & had her letters A.T.C.L. even taught music for a short time. We took over the Temperance Hotel in Clinton on the 1st July 1939 Just before the 2nd WORLD WAR. No electric power or Licence for drink in Clinton

Grandma, when you were little what was bedtime like in your family? Did your parents ever read stories or sing to you?

"They were too busy to spend time reading to us and we would just go to bed and talk and then sleep. We had jobs to do; washing floors and doorsteps. We would also wait on tables at lunchtime and teatime."

Grandma, what are the things you value most in life?

"We had great friends and neighbours. We would help each other out with the children.

We had the most amazing holidays together with friends and family, and I am extremely grateful and love them all so very much.

Grandma, what's an important lesson your parents taught you, something you've tried to live by and share with your own kids?

 "Never tell lies and treat your elders with respect."

Grandma, what are the secrets of staying young at heart?

"Keeping yourself busy working at what you can do well."

I will always remember my mum fondly and especially for the one month of her life she dedicated to completing her book.

She will be remembered as a Proverbs 31:10-12 woman.

> *A wife of noble character who can find?*
> *She is worth far more than rubies.*
> *Her husband has full confidence in her*
> *and lacks nothing of value.*
> *She brings him good, not harm,*
> *all the days of her life.*

She has left a legacy for generations to follow.

What kind of legacy do you want to leave?

Writing a book

Earlier this year I was walking along the beach in Pegasus, where I now live, and heard God speak to me. I was listening to a podcast from Alan Scott of Anaheim Vineyard: "When we leave this planet the most powerful thing we leave here are our stories."

I felt God say that I needed to write a book about my stories. This is how *Journey in Wonder* came about.

The key to living an abundant life is being thankful and having a willingness to help others.

My life has been blessed through the people I have met, relationships built, and wonders and discoveries along the way. I can look back on an abundance of opportunity and I know there is more to come.

I have seen some fruit from the things I have been involved in. However, I also realise some of the fruit of my life will not be seen in my lifetime. It will sit like a buried treasure, undiscovered, waiting for the right moment to reveal itself, and hopefully inspire another generation.

I hope this book has encouraged you. I hope it helps you to get closer to God, to pursue a dream, to heal a past hurt and encourage others more. And, lastly, may it help to birth the seeds God has planted within you so you bear much fruit.

By the way, my father found those ratty fawn trousers three weeks later, hidden in a bottom drawer, with some of my mum's underwear.